THE MEANINGS OF GANDHI

THE
MEANINGS OF GANDHI
Edited by Paul F. Power

AN EAST-WEST CENTER BOOK
The University Press of Hawaii

Frontispiece
Brush drawing by Ben Shahn, 1964
Courtesy of John D. Rockefeller 3rd

Abel

CONTENTS

THE MEANINGS OF GANDHI

INTRODUCTION

There are many evaluations of the life and ideas of Mohandas K. Gandhi. Some observers have found that he was a moral teacher of timeless and universal importance. This is the opinion of Sarvepalli Radhakrishnan, the philosopher and former President of India. In contrast, others like Reinhold Niebuhr have argued that Gandhi's significance is restricted to the culture and period in which he lived. Many liberal reformers in Asia and the West have praised him as an ongoing inspirational and tactical resource for efforts to eliminate racism and war. However, Marxists like R. Palme Dutt have criticized Gandhi for endorsing nonviolence instead of revolutionary class struggle to end economic injustice. Third World sympathizers of varied political ideologies have credited Gandhi for his early and effective contributions to furthering the collective dignity and national independence of colonial peoples. Yet some have rejected, as did George Orwell, his teachings about sexual matters. A Muslim intellectual like Humayun Kabir could applaud Gandhi as a religious pluralist whereas a Hindu nationalist like V. D. Savarkar condemned him for denying Hindu primacy. Some who have grown to maturity since Gandhi's assassination in 1948 and who question industrial

society and state policies have welcomed his attachment to village
self-reliance and civil disobedience. But with all of these varying
and sometimes divergent evaluations, there has been and there is
today striking agreement that Gandhi was an extraordinary
person and national leader whose impact is still felt and will be
felt for decades to come in many parts of the world.

A special opportunity to reexamine the thought and career of
Gandhi came during 1969, the centenary of his birth. UNESCO,
many governments and universities, and private groups marked
the occasion. As part of the centennial activities, a symposium was
held in November at the Center for Cultural and Technical Inter-
change between East and West, University of Hawaii, Honolulu.
Organized by the Gandhi Centennial Committee of the Committee on South Asia of the Association for Asian Studies, of
which I was privileged to be chairman, the five-day meeting
brought together scholars of different training and outlook. Some
had known or worked with Gandhi. Aware of the achievements
as well as the shortcomings of Gandhian studies, the participants
reassessed Gandhi's assumptions and ideas, his influence on his
own country and time, and his bequest to other places and generations. Supported by the Association for Asian Studies and assisted
by the Watumull Foundation, the symposium was made possible
by the generosity of the East-West Center. On behalf of the participants, I wish to express appreciation to these three institutions
for their aid to the project. Papers prepared for the meeting,
chaired by Professor Richard L. Park of the University of Michi-
gan, form the basis for this book.

Gandhi's creativity as a person and a public actor is treated
in the volume's first section. During his long and eventful life
which spanned the Victorian and Atomic periods and saw his
involvement in high policy matters in South Africa, Britain, and
India, Gandhi had special relations with a number of people.
Some influenced his premises and conduct. Among them were
Kasturba, Gandhi's wife, and the Jain poet and jeweler, Ray-
chandbhai, who may have been a crucial factor in persuading
Gandhi to remain a Hindu. With others, like his political oppo-

nents, Jan Christian Smuts of South Africa and Lord Irwin, the Viceroy with whom he negotiated as an equal to the dismay of Winston Churchill, conflict was followed by mutual respect.

The book begins with an analysis of the especially important relationship between Gandhi and Jawaharlal Nehru. Mr. Bal Ram Nanda, Director of the Nehru Memorial Museum and Library in New Delhi and a biographer of Gandhi and the Nehrus, places Gandhi and Nehru within the complexities of Indian nationalism. He examines the intricate bonds of sentiment and purpose which created a working partnership between the two and explores the question of whether their philosophies ever converged. In the second study, Professor Susanne Hoeber Rudolph of the University of Chicago analyzes the sources of Gandhi's power of attracting as political or financial supporters men so different as Vallabhbhai Patel and G. D. Birla. Mrs. Rudolph suggests that Gandhi's followership rested on para-kinship ties and his ability to relate aspects of his program to constituent personality and interest. The next essay takes the discussion of Gandhi the public actor into the wider framework of the struggle of the Indian National Congress with British imperialism. Professor Ainslie T. Embree of Duke University critically explores Gandhi's impact on the earlier and later stages of the nationalist movement and his contribution to the search for national identity and integration by means of a transcendent ideology.

Mr. Embree's mention of the growth and fulfillment of Muslim separatism within Indian anticolonialism evokes the question as to whether Gandhi—despite his work for Hindu-Muslim unity and against the Muslim League's two-nation theory—had any responsibility for developments leading to partition in 1947 and the creation of Pakistan. In the Honolulu meeting, Dr. Nirmal Kumar Bose, a secretary to Gandhi and later India's Commissioner for Scheduled Castes and Tribes, commented that when partition and Hindu-Muslim genocide emerged, Gandhi believed that all parties had become communalistic, requiring that he and India start again.

The second part of the book concerns Gandhi's ideas and

their transmission. Dr. Bose explains the origins of *sarvodaya* and how this vision of social justice is meant to remedy social and economic problems faced by Gandhi and after him by Vinoba and Jayaprakash Narayan who have tried to solve them through the Land-Gift Movement. Dr. Bose evaluates problems of organization and self-criticism which he believes Gandhians fail to answer as they attempt to reform the intricate Indian society for which the central government has its own, different plans.

Subsequently, a central Gandhian value, ahimsa or non-violence, is analyzed by Professor Karl H. Potter of the University of Minnesota. Reviewing classical Hindu and Western pacifist interpretations of violence, he rejects the widely held opinion that Gandhi's ideas forbid both spiritual-psychological violence and physical injury, and he suggests that Gandhi's absolutist condemnation of war was out of character with the overall structure of his thought. This section closes with an analysis of Indian foreign policy in the perspective of Gandhi's teachings by Professor Werner Levi of the University of Hawaii. He evaluates Gandhi's expectations for his country's external conduct after freedom and the relationship of Gandhian values to the nature of world politics. That Gandhi recognized that there is a constant tension between political reality and moral idealism is a reminder of a basic issue in any nation's diplomacy.

The relative importance of Gandhi cannot be known without comparative insights. The book's third and concluding section provides several. Professor Donald E. Smith of the University of Pennsylvania opens with a comparison of Gandhi and two other value-laden activists, Vinoba and Camilo Torres, the Columbian cleric. Mr. Smith uses the criteria of mass mobilization, a strategy of conflict, and concrete goals to evaluate Gandhi's relative standing as a religious revolutionary. The Smith essay raises a broader question about Gandhi: does the character of the man and his work require that he should always be treated in part as a religious figure?

Estimates of Gandhi must take into account the idea of satyagraha and its techniques of reform. This is done in the essay on Gandhian values within the American civil rights movement by Dr. William Stuart Nelson, vice president emeritus of Howard University. Calling attention to the historical importance of American supporters of pacifism, he reviews personal and intellectual contacts between Gandhi and black Christian spokesmen and appraises Black Power in the light of Gandhian teachings. Gandhi's version of civil disobedience is the subject of my paper which examines his premises and his ethics of rule-breaking and the way in which they may contribute to the advancement of conflict and conflict resolution. I point out Gandhi's elitist answer to the question of who is authorized to call for disobedience, his weak treatment of citizenship, and the differences between his understanding of resistance to state policies and unjust laws and that of the New Left. The final essay returns the discussions to higher levels of generality by means of a comparison of two apparent unlikes, Gandhi and Machiavelli. Professor Anthony Parel of the University of Calgary probes their interpretations of man, the world, and first values. As theorists and practitioners, both Gandhi and Machiavelli saw politics as energy and the interplay of ethical and power variables, but they differed on the way to reform. Together they accounted for comprehensive political action.

These essays are not meant to answer the many questions that can be raised about Gandhi. What they do attempt to provide are clearer and, in some instances, new explanations for several issues that have troubled Gandhi's critics and which his partisans have not always faced. The authors hope that they have expanded knowledge about the Indian leader, his country, and his legacy for resolving problems common to most men and nations.

Paul F. Power

University of Cincinnati
March, 1971

GANDHI THE MAN AND
PUBLIC ACTOR

1

GANDHI AND NEHRU

Bal Ram Nanda

How two men, divided not only by twenty years of age but by deep intellectual and tempermental differences, could work together for so long is an enigma for anyone who seriously studies the lives of Gandhi and Nehru and the history of their times. Jawaharlal Nehru, the young aristocrat from Allahabad, seemed to have little in common with the strange charismatic figure who burst upon the Indian political stage in 1919 with an almost elemental force. The primary school in Porbandar where young Gandhi wrote the alphabet in dust with his fingers and the Bhavnagar college where he painfully struggled with lectures in English belonged to an altogether different world from that of European governesses and resident tutors in Allahabad, Harrow, Cambridge and the Inns of Court in England in which young Nehru matured. True, Gandhi also went to England to study for the bar in the late 1880's. But young Gandhi poring over the Bible and the Gita and desperately fighting back the recurring temptation of "wine, woman and meat" was cast in an altogether different mould from that of the handsome Kashmiri youth, clad in Savile Row elegance, who prided himself on his agnosticism and "cyrenaicism," who frequented the theatre and admired Oscar Wilde and Walter Pater, and who dabbled in Irish politics and Fabian economics. In the course of his twenty-odd years stay in South Africa, Gandhi fashioned for himself a peculiar, almost unique philosophy of life which, though baffling to many of his contemporaries, was firmly grounded in deeply-held convictions.

How could Jawaharlal Nehru with his enthusiasm for science and humanism feel kinship with a saint preoccupied with prayers and fasts, inner voices and the spinning wheel? This is a question to which biographers, historians and political commentators will continue to seek answers. Percival Spear has suggested that Jawaharlal had a compulsive need to depend on someone, that at first the mentor was his father Motilal and then Gandhi.[1] M. N. Roy suspected that Jawaharlal's mind was a slave to his heart, that he deliberately suppressed his own personality "to purchase popularity" and become "the hero of Indian nationalism . . . as the spiritual son of Gandhi."[2] Hiren Mukerjee has hazarded the theory that Gandhi won over and astutely kept Jawaharlal on his side to exploit his charisma and influence with India's youth in the interest of the Congress party which was in reality controlled by vested interests.[3] These interpretations have the merit of simplicity, but they do not fit the facts of a partnership which extended over nearly three decades. The story of this partnership, the strains to which it was subjected and the factors which enabled it to survive, show that it was not simply a case of domination of one by the other, that Jawaharlal needed Gandhi as much as Gandhi needed him, that political calculation no less than emotional affinity kept them together during these years.

When Gandhi returned to India at the age of forty-five early in 1915, his personality had already taken shape. To his Western-educated contemporaries he seemed an eccentric specimen of an English-educated Indian. His South African record had given him a halo, but in the shadow of the Great War, public opinion was worried less about the Indian minority in South Africa than about India's political future. Gandhi's view that unconditional support to the British war effort would earn its reward from a grateful Empire in the hour of victory seemed to most of his contemporaries extraordinarily naive. And, as if this were not enough, Gandhi also harped on the superiority of Indian over Western civilization and denounced industrialism in favor of village handicrafts. All this must have sounded strangely unpolitical and anachronistic to Jawaharlal Nehru who had returned to India in 1912 after a seven-year sojourn in England. Though he had seen Gandhi at the Bombay Congress in 1915 and again at Lucknow a year later, Jawaharlal was not really attracted to him until after the Champaran and Kaira campaigns and the anti-Rowlatt Bill agitation. There were good reasons why Gandhi's satyagraha campaigns should have made an impact on Jawaharlal. Seven years at the Allahabad High Court, as his father's junior, had left Jawaharlal bored with the trivialities and technicalities of the legal profession. The game of making money did not excite him. He was groping for a new *weltanschauung*. Political terrorism had little attraction for him. The annual sessions of the Indian National Congress and the arm-chair politics with which the elite of Allahabad amused itself seemed to him much too tame. He was drawn to Gokhale's Servants of India Society with its band of political sannyasins, but he was repelled by its association with moderate politics. When Gandhi published the satyagraha pledge and announced direct action to protest against the Rowlatt Bills, Jawaharlal was thrilled by the prospect of effective political action.

Motilal Nehru did not find it easy to reconcile himself to extra-constitutional agitation, but Gandhi counselled him to be patient. Soon afterwards, in the aftermath of the tragedy of martial law in the Punjab, Motilal came into closer contact with Gandhi and was surprised to find in him not a starry-eyed saint but a politician with a keen practical sense.[4] Before long the whole Nehru family came under the Mahatma's spell and learned to seek solace and support from the saint of Sabarmati. This was an emotional bond independent of politics but not without its influence on the political life of India. Differences of ideology and tactics become a little less intractable when there is a reserve of mutual respect and affection.

Gandhi's first impact on young Nehru was pronounced. He said that he was "simply bowled over by Gandhi straight off."[5] The call to nonviolent battle against the British Raj in 1919-20 struck a chord. "I jumped to it. I did not care for the consequences." His life underwent a metamorphosis. He turned his back on the legal profession, simplified his life, gave up smoking, became a vegetarian and began to read the Gita regularly, "not from a philosophical or theological point of view," but because "it had numerous parts which had a powerful effect upon me."[6] He was fired by the missionary fervor of a new convert. "Non-cooperation is to me," he wrote to the Chief Secretary to the United Provinces Government, "a sacred thing and its very basis is truth and non-violence."[7] He was full of excitement, optimism, and buoyant enthusiasm. He sensed "the happiness of a person crusading for a cause." He was so wholly absorbed by the movement that he "gave up all other associations and contacts, old friends, books, even newspapers except in so far as they dealt with the work in hand . . . I almost forgot my family, my wife, my daughter."[8]

A rude awakening from this ecstasy occurred in February 1922. After a riot at Chauri Chaura in the United Provinces, Gandhi called off civil disobedience. In prison at the time, Jawaharlal received the news with amazement and consternation. He did not see how the violence of a stray mob of excited peasants in a remote village could justify the reversal of a national struggle for freedom. If perfect nonviolence was to be regarded as a sine qua non for all the three hundred-odd million Indians would it not reduce Gandhi's movement to a pious futility? A letter from Gandhi somewhat mollified Jawaharlal, but it was only much later, with the perspective that time gives, that he realized that Gandhi's decision was right.

The Chauri Chaura tragedy brought Jawaharlal down to earth. The exaltation of the non-cooperation days faded away. He had no stomach for the factional and communal politics of the mid-1920's. He served as Allahabad's Mayor and as General Secretary of the All India Congress Committee. These activities provided useful outlets for his boundless energy, but he did not recover his zest for politics and indeed for life until he visited Europe during 1926-27 for the treatment of his ailing wife. Under the stimulus of fresh reading and contacts with revolutionaries and radicals of three continents, the realization dawned on him that Indian politics had been much too vague, narrow and parochial. He learned to trace links not only between British imperialism in India and colonialism in other countries of Asia and Africa, but also between foreign domination and vested interests in his own country. The Brussels Congress of Oppressed Nationalities and his brief visit to the Soviet Union gave a tremendous impetus to these ideas. On return to the homeland in December 1927, he persuaded the Madras Congress to pass resolutions in favor of complete independence. He denounced feudalism, capitalism and imperialism and talked of organizing workers, peasants and students.

Jawaharlal's performance at the Madras Congress deeply disturbed Gandhi. He wrote to Jawaharlal:

> You are going too fast; you should have taken time to think and become acclimatised. Most of the resolutions you prepared and got carried could have been delayed for one year. Your plunging into the "republican army" was a hasty step. But I do not mind these acts of yours so much as I mind your encouraging mischief makers and hooligans. . . . If . . . careful observation of the country in the light of your European experiences convinces you of the error of the current ways and means, by all means enforce your own views, but do please form a disciplined party.[9]

Gandhi's objection was not so much to the radical views of the younger man as to the light-hearted manner in which brave declarations were made without any serious effort to implement them. It was all very well to talk of complete independence, but did the Indian people have the will to enforce such a demand? "We have almost sunk to the level of a school boys' debating society," the Mahatma told Jawaharlal. A few months later, he told Motilal Nehru, who headed the committee which was to draft an All-Parties Constitution (The Nehru Report), that "unless we have created some force ourselves, we shall not advance beyond the position of beggars. . . . We are not ready for drawing up a constitution till we have developed a sanction for ourselves."[10] The only sanction that Gandhi could forge was that provided by a nonviolent struggle.

In December 1928, when the advocates of independence and dominion status clashed at the Calcutta Congress, Jawaharlal is reported to have told Gandhi: "Bapu, the difference between you and me is this: you believe in gradualism; I stand for revolution." "My dear young man," Gandhi retorted, "I have made revolutions while others have only shouted revolutions. When your lungs are exhausted and you really are serious about it you will come to me and I shall then show you how a revolution is made."[11] After a long heated argument, much vacillation and mental distress, Jawaharlal eventually fell into line with Gandhi's compromise formula. Dominion status was accepted as the basis of the new constitution, provided the British Government conceded it before the end of 1929.

To many of his young admirers Jawaharlal's attitude at the Calcutta Congress smacked of political cowardice; to Subhas Bose and members of the Independence for India League it seemed an abject betrayal. But it was a sound instinct which kept Jawaharlal from breaking with the Congress Old Guard and the Mahatma. He seems to have sensed that if there were any conservatives at the Calcutta Congress, Gandhi was not one of them. As events were to prove, it was Jawaharlal, not the old Guard, who won at Calcutta. There were some apparent disappointments and setbacks such as the issues of the Delhi Manifesto, the Viceroy's statement, and the peace parleys in Delhi just before the Lahore Congress. Nevertheless, the fact remained that within a year "complete independence" became the battle-cry of the Congress

party, and Gandhi was back at its helm to direct another satyagraha struggle against the British Raj. Jawaharlal was delighted.

After the Calcutta Congress the political atmosphere became electric. Gandhi abandoned a trip to Europe which he had
been planning and called for a boycott of foreign cloth. Rumors
circulated of Jawaharlal's imminent arrest as he threw himself
into the organizational work of the Congress with redoubled
vigor. Politics again acquired for him a sense of purpose, urgency,
and adventure. All the signs pointed to Gandhi's return to active
leadership of the party. A majority of the provincial Congress
committees voted for him to preside over the Lahore session in
December 1929. Gandhi declined the honor, but persuaded the
All India Congress Committee to confer it on Jawaharlal. Admission to the highest office in the Congress by a "trapdoor [which
had] bewildered the audience into acceptance"[12] was humiliating
to Nehru. Nevertheless, his good fortune in presiding over the
momentous session at Lahore and in unfurling the flag of independence on the bank of the Ravi at midnight on December 31, 1929,
rocketed his prestige overnight. The Lahore Congress gave a
tremendous boost to Jawaharlal's popularity with the masses. It
raised his stock with the intelligentsia and made him a hero of
India's youth.

As the new year dawned events moved fast. With the
observance of Independence Day and the launching of the Salt
Satyagraha, the political scene began to be transformed under the
magic touch of the Mahatma. And once again, in the midst of
a struggle against the British, Jawaharlal felt that sense of complete identification with Gandhi which he had experienced ten
years before. The Salt Satyagraha drew the whole Nehru family
into the arena. Jawaharlal was the first to be arrested. He was
followed by his father, his sisters and his wife. But once again
history repeated itself, and Gandhi called off the movement when
it seemed to be on the crest of a rising wave. Nehru was in Delhi
in February and March 1931 and in touch with the Mahatma
during his talks with the Viceroy. Nevertheless, the content of
the Gandhi-Irwin Pact of March 4, particularly its second clause

concerning safeguards in the new constitution, came as a great
shock to Jawaharlal.

> So I lay and pondered on that March night and in my heart
> there was a great emptiness as of something precious gone,
> almost beyond recall. . . . The thing had been done, our
> leader had committed himself; and even if we disagreed with
> him, what could we do? Throw him over? Break from him?
> Announce our disagreement? That might bring some personal
> satisfaction to an individual, but it made no difference to the
> final decision.[13]

Gandhi observed Jawaharlal's distress, took him out for a
walk, and tried to allay his fears. Jawaharlal was not convinced,
but at the Karachi Congress, a few days later, he swallowed his
dissent and even sponsored the resolution supporting the Gandhi-
Irwin Pact. He was motivated by a desire to prevent an open
rift in the party and to strengthen the hands of Gandhi who was
to represent the Congress at the Round Table Conference in
London.

In December 1931, when Gandhi returned from his abor-
tive trip to London, Jawaharlal was already in jail. The Gandhi-
Irwin Pact soon went to pieces, civil disobedience was resumed,
the Congress was outlawed and more than sixty thousand persons
were convicted for civil disobedience. Jawaharlal had one of his
longest spells in jail—a total of 1,170 days—between December
1931 and September 1935. It was towards the close of this period
that he wrote his autobiography. The author's preface referred
to the "mood of self-questioning" and the "particularly distress-
ful period" of his life in which the book was written. The
distress stemmed not only from anxiety about his wife, who was
hovering between life and death in Indian and Swiss sanatoria,
but also from the decline of the struggle against the British Raj.
As he recalled the story of his life and the course of the movement
to which he had given his all, Jawaharlal noted the conflicting

pulls which Gandhi exerted on him. Despite his admiration for the Mahatma, Nehru found much in Gandhi which puzzled and even infuriated him. When he learned about Gandhi's fast against separate electorates for the depressed classes, he felt angry with the Mahatma's religious and sentimental approach to a political question.

The untouchability fast was not the only occasion when Gandhi's religious idiom jarred Nehru. In 1934, the Mahatma suggested that the terrible earthquake which Bihar had just suffered was a divine punishment for the sin of untouchability. It struck Nehru as a "staggering remark . . . anything more opposed to scientific outlook it would be difficult to imagine."[14] A few months later Gandhi's statement, while calling off civil disobedience, left him gasping with its emotional irrelevance. Jawaharlal had a "sudden and intense feeling that something broke inside me, a bond that I had valued very greatly had snapped. I felt terribly lonely in this wide world. . . . Again I felt that sensation of spiritual isolation, of being a perfect stranger out of harmony, not only with the crowds that passed me, but also with those whom I had valued as dear and close comrades."[15]

On occasions Gandhi struck Jawaharlal as a medieval Catholic saint. Gandhi's philosophy of "one step enough for me" seemed to him much too empirical, his political style too abrupt and unpredictable, his doctrine of nonviolence too lofty for the common run of mankind. Nehru's autobiography reflects his doubts and self-questioning and mental conflict. He asked whether nonviolence was not hardening into dogma and assuming a place, alongside other religious doctrines, as a cover for vested interests. Was it not an illusion, he speculated, to imagine that an imperialist power would give up its domination over a country or that a class would give up its superior position and privileges unless effective pressure amounting to coercion were exercised? Was it not romantic to hope for the conversion of princes, landlords and capitalists into trustees of their properties for the commonweal or to expect khadi and village industries to solve the long-term problem of India's poverty? Was not Gandhi's emphasis on the spinning wheel overdone and foredoomed to failure in an industrialized world?

These doubts assailed Jawaharlal as he wrote his autobiography. Some found expression in his talks with Gandhi in 1933 when he was briefly out of jail. While Nehru was detained during the next two years, his differences with the Mahatma sharpened. A band of young Congressmen, disillusioned by the failure of civil disobedience and attracted to socialist doctrines, took up Nehru's ideas. In the 1920's, the young radicals had challenged the Congress elite on political issues such as dominion status versus independence. In the 1930's, they challenged the leadership on economic as well as political issues. The contest was to be more serious not only for the coherence of the Congress party but for relations between Nehru and Gandhi. Their association at this time cannot be understood without noting their diverse social philosophies.

Though Jawaharlal had sampled Fabian literature and attended Bernard Shaw's lectures as a student in Cambridge and London, he derived his enthusiasm for Marxism and the Russian Revolution from reading and reflection in jail and his visit to Europe in 1926-27 which had included a four-day trip to Moscow. It is significant that one of the aims of the Independence of India League, which he and Subhas Bose had founded in 1928, was the revision of the economic structure of society on a socialist basis. In his presidential address at the Lahore Congress, Jawaharlal avowed himself a socialist. A little earlier he had presided over the All India Trade Union Congress where he argued that despite the bourgeois character of the Congress, it did represent the only effective force in the country. In March 1931, thanks largely to Gandhi's support, he urged the Karachi Congress resolution on fundamental rights and economic policy which envisaged, among other things, the state ownership of key industries and services, mineral resources, railways, waterways and shipping and other means of transport. According to J. B. Kripalani, it was the powerful backing of Gandhi which caused the Congress leadership to accept the resolution.[16] It is true that this resolution was only mildly socialistic, but socialist ideas had not yet gained much currency in the Congress. It was not until 1934 that young Congressmen in Nasik jail, who shared disenchantment with Gandhi's leadership, formed a socialist party. Among them were Jayaprakash Narayan, Asoka Mehta, Achyut Patwardhan and Yusuf Meherally. They were later joined by Narendra Deva, Sri Prakasa, Sampurnananda, N. G. Ranga and others. They swore by Marxism, talked of the inevitability of class war, and called for planned economic development on the Soviet model. They discounted Gandhi's leadership as well as the efficacy of nonviolence in solving Indian political and social problems. They made Gandhi their target. As socialists, they believed that it was only by drawing in the masses, peasants, and workers that Congress could broaden its base, rid itself of its defeatist mentality," "socialize the nationalist struggle," and forge a massive anti-imperialist front.[17]

Gandhi was not impressed by the political wisdom of these young men. Their talk of class war, expropriation and violence displeased him. Nevertheless—and this was characteristic of Gandhi—he refused to be a party to the muzzling of Congress socialists. Indeed, he helped them to secure a larger representation in the All India Congress Committee by the introduction of the single transferable vote. He also announced his own formal retirement from the Congress organization so that his critics, including the young socialists, should be able to express their views without being inhibited by his presence.

In jail when the Congress Socialist party began, Nehru did not become an office-bearer or even a member of the group. But there is no doubt that he was its hero and a source of inspiration. Some leaders of the party, such as Narendra Deva, Jayaprakash Narayan and Achyut Patwardhan, were close to Nehru and shared his outlook on national and international issues. However, Nehru's socialism was never doctrinaire. Nor did he plan "to inoculate the masses with the virus of communism," as the Government of India suspected.[18] "I am certainly a socialist," he wrote in March 1938. "I believe in the socialist theory and method of approach. I am not a Communist chiefly because I resist the Communist tendency to treat Communism as holy doctrine and I do not like being told what to think and what to do."[19] He made no secret of his faith in scientific socialism. He believed in curbing the profit motive, in promoting public ownership of key industries, and in using the machinery of the state to regulate economic activity. Gandhi's approach was different.

When not yet forty Gandhi had developed a social philosophy of his own based on a faith in nonviolence and a distrust of industrialism and the modern state. Gandhi's utopia, a federation of small village republics, would provide only for the essential needs of the community. Based on a thorough-going decentralization of the economic and political structures, it would reduce the temptation for internal exploitation and external aggression. This philosophy imitated neither British nor Soviet modes but was tailored to Indian conditions. It was to be, in Gandhi's words, *Ram Rajya*. Congress socialists did not take seriously the Mahatma's claim to be a socialist. To them, as to Nehru, the Mahatma's socialism was "a kind of muddled humanitarianism."[20]

Imprisonment and domestic affliction kept Jawaharlal out of Indian politics for nearly four and a half years. Curiously enough, while he was behind prison bars, his political stock had risen. His name became well known among the masses as well as the intelligentsia. Nehru's autobiography soon gave him a world-wide reputation. Gandhi knew of Nehru's popularity as well as his differences with the Congress leadership. In spite of the latter, Gandhi secured Nehru's election to the presidency of the 1936 Congress. Conscious of the fact that the socialists were a small minority Nehru included only three of them—Jayaprakash Narayan, Achyut Patwardhan and Narendra Deva—in the Congress Working Committee, and he gave the remaining eleven seats to the Old Guard including Gandhiites. The Committee found it hard to socialize. The political temperature rose, and it was heightened by Nehru's militant address at the Lucknow Congress.

The Congress socialists seemed anxious to drive their advantage home. The older leaders were suspicious and nervous. Nehru himself was on edge. "Today I feel," he wrote to a friend on May 3, 1936, "that there could be "a severe tug-of-war in India between rival ideologies. . . . I feel myself very much on the side of one ideology and I am distressed at some of my colleagues going the other way."[21] Two days later he wrote about his sense of intellectual isolation in the Working Committee. "The last dozen years . . . have been years of hard and continuous work for me, of self-education and study and thought. . . . But others . . . have not taken the trouble to think or study and have remained vaguely where they were. But the world changes."[22] By the end of June, the crisis, unknown to the public, came to a head when seven members of the Congress Working Committee sent their resignations to Nehru.

Not only ideological differences, but also conflicting readings of the political situation, brought on the crisis in the Congress executive. Perhaps even more important was the mistrust between the Old Guard and the Congress Socialists. Each feared being edged out of the party. Nehru suspected that there was a conspiracy to destroy him politically. Gandhi was not, of course, a party to such a plot. Indeed, he resolved the crisis with admirable speed, skill and firmness. He insisted on the withdrawal of the resignations and vetoed the reference of the dispute to the All India Congress Committee on the ground that a public discussion would only aggravate and distort the differences among the leaders, confuse and demoralize the rank and file, and ruin the party's chances at the election. Though as late as November 1936 Edward Thompson was predicting that the Congress would split and "Nehru will lead a group into the wilderness,"[23] the crisis was really over.

Nehru was prudent enough not to heed the advice of the hotheads among his admirers who were urging him to extreme courses. If he had broken with Gandhi and the Congress in 1936, he would have dealt a blow not only to the Congress but to his own political future. It was obvious that so long as Gandhi re-

mained at the helm of the Congress, it was unlikely that any
rival nationalist party could emerge or compete with it. The
founding or even the running of a political party was not Nehru's
métier. He could sway crowds, inspire intellectuals, reel off press
statements and articles, run the AICC office and travel from one
end of the country to the other, but he was not cut out for the role
of a party manager. He did not have Gandhi's gift for discovering,
training and harnessing to the national cause men and women of
varying abilities and temperaments. "I function individually," he
told Subhas Bose, "without any group or any second person to
support me."[24] Admirable in its own way, this detachment
limited his room for maneuver within the party. When Bose
remonstrated with Nehru for not supporting him against Gandhi,
Nehru frankly said that a head-on collision with the Mahatma
was likely to be suicidal. "The Left," he warned Bose, "was not
strong enough to shoulder the burden by itself, and when a real
contest came in the Congress, it would lose and then there would
be a reaction against it." Bose could win the election and become
Congress president against Pattabhi Sitaramayya, but Nehru
doubted whether Bose could carry the Congress in a clear contest
with what was called Gandhiism. Even if he won a majority
within the Congress, it would not ensure Bose a sufficient backing
in the country. And in any case a mass struggle against the government without Gandhi was inconceivable. Finally, Nehru warned
Bose that there were many "disruptive tendencies" already in the
country, and it was not right to add to them and to weaken the
national movement.[25]

During this crisis Gandhi revealed with remarkable candor
his reasons for supporting Nehru's candidacy for the Congress
presidency in 1936, even though Nehru's ideas were in conflict
with those of a majority of his colleagues in the party leadership.
"You are in office," wrote Gandhi to Jawaharlal on July 15, 1936,
"by their unanimous choice, but you are not in power yet. To
put you in office was an attempt to put you in power quicker than
you would otherwise have been. Anyway that was at the back of
my mind when I suggested your name for the Crown of thorns."[26]

Thus it is clear that Nehru's elevation to the Congress presidency in 1936 was not, as Hiren Mukerjee suggests, to imprison the socialist wave "in a strong little reservoir" of Gandhi's own making,[27] but to launch him in a favorable wind on the wide and stormy ocean of Indian politics.

It is true that in 1936-37 Nehru could not have his way on two crucial issues—elections to the new legislatures and the formation of Congress ministries. But, due to Nehru's influence, the decisions on these issues did not dampen Indian nationalism. The Congress election manifesto bore marks of Nehru's militant socialism and anti-imperialism. And the election campaign, largely because of his prominent part in it, had the effect of awakening the masses. Finally, when the Congress accepted office, it was on its own terms, not on those of the British Government. The continual criticisms from Nehru and his socialist friends had the salutary effect of preventing the Congress ministries from sliding into bureaucratic grooves. Thus, Nehru's presidency gave a radical twist to Congress politics in 1936-37. Even E. M. S. Namboodiripad acknowledges that the presence of a left-wing leader at the head of the Congress "enormously strengthened the forces of the left, the ideas of socialism, of militant and uncompromising anti-imperialism, of anti-landlord and anti-capitalist struggles . . . began to grip the people on a scale never before thought possible."[28]

In 1936, as in 1928, Nehru had stooped to Gandhi, but he had stooped to conquer. It is true that he was not able to get his views and programs accepted immediately or in their entirety, but he was able to influence the final decisions much more from within the party than he would have been able to do if, like Subhas Bose, he had left it to plough his own lonely furrow. Thanks to Gandhi's intervention, the 1936 crisis in the Congress passed. Jawaharlal continued to be the president and was in fact re-elected for another year. He was not in tune, however, with his colleagues in the Working Committee. Gandhi sensed Nehru's unhappiness and irascibility. The Mahatma would often seek Nehru's approbation for whatever he was doing.

The differences between the two men during these years were often on current issues, representing a difference of approach or emphasis. Nehru, for instance, was not happy about Gandhi's interview with the Governor of Bengal on the release of the détenus or about the embargo on Congress participation in popular agitation in the princely states. The slow implementation of the reforms by the Congress ministries vexed him, while most of his colleagues felt that he did not make a sufficient allowance for the limitations under which they worked. The activities of the Congress socialists provided another cause for misunderstanding. Some of them who were close to Nehru made no secret of their conviction that Gandhi was played out, that he was incapable of giving further leadership against the British, that his technique of nonviolence could not take the country to the final goal. After reading a book on the Russian Revolution, Rafi Ahmed Kidwai confided to Nehru: "If we want to make further progress, we will have to make an attempt to destroy the mentality created by the C. D. [Civil disobedience]. . . . We will have to give up the present standards of scrupulousness, personal integrity, honesty and political amiability."[29] Narendra Deva and Jayaprakash Narayan had similar criticisms to make of Gandhi. It is not unlikely that what his friends were saying reflected Nehru's own inner misgivings at this time. The intellectual hiatus between him and Gandhi tended to blow up even small tactical differences into minor crises.

The outbreak of war in September 1939 added yet another strand to a complex situation. It set into motion forces which transformed not only party alignments in India but the structure of power in the world. It also revealed a fundamental cleavage between Gandhi and Nehru in their attitudes toward the war. "Perhaps this is the most critical period in our history," Gandhi wrote to Nehru on October 26, 1939. "I hold very strong views on the most important questions which occupy our attention. I know you too hold strong views on them but different from mine. Your mode of expression is different from mine."[30]

Nehru had been publicly hailed by Gandhi as his guide on international affairs. At Nehru's insistence the Congress had denounced Fascist aggression in Manchuria, Abyssinia, Spain and Czechoslovakia and had taken the Western powers to task for their policy of appeasement toward the dictators. Nevertheless, Nehru had a lurking feeling that Gandhi had often accepted his viewpoint on international affairs without wholly agreeing with it. The Mahatma was second to none in his hatred of the tyrannies set up by the Fascist and Nazi regimes. He regarded Nazism and Fascism as symptoms of a deep-seated disease—the cult of violence. Yet he did not believe that violence could be neutralized by counter-violence. Through the pages of his weekly paper, the *Harijan,* he exhorted the victims of aggression to defend themselves with nonviolent resistance. Even after Hitler had overrun Poland in 1939 and Europe was gripped by fear and foreboding, the Mahatma continued to affirm that nonviolence could serve as an effective shield against aggression.

Neither Nehru, nor the majority of the members of the Congress Working Committee, nor indeed the rank and file of the party, shared Gandhi's boundless faith in the efficacy of nonviolence. Clearly Nehru did not view the war as an occasion for asserting the power of the concept. He did not believe that nonviolence would destroy the monstrous war-machine built by Hitler before it could enslave mankind. Nehru had never accepted nonviolence as a method for all situations or all times.

It soon became obvious that behind the facade of unity, the Congress leaders had serious differences in their approach to the war. The primary motivation of radicals like Jayaprakash Narayan was anti-British, of Nehru anti-Fascist, and of Gandhi anti-war. These differences would have come sharply into focus if the British Government under the influence of Churchill and Linlithgow had not shortsightedly tried to freeze the constitutional position for the duration of the conflict. So long as there was no question of effective Congress participation in the central government, the question whether India's support to the Allies was to be moral (as Gandhi advocated) or military (as Nehru proposed) remained purely academic. On two occasions the vicissitudes of war seemed to bring a rapprochement between the Congress and the Government within the realm of practical politics. In 1940, after the French collapse and in 1941-42, after the Japanese triumph in Southeast Asia, Gandhi found that the majority of his colleagues were ready to switch from a pacifist stand to a whole-hearted participation in the Allied war effort in return for a reciprocal gesture by the British Government.

The period immediately preceding and following the Cripps Mission in 1942 was a testing time for Jawaharlal. He had little love for the British Government, but he was dismayed by its obstinate refusal to read the writing on the wall. Meanwhile, Indian public opinion reached the height of frustration. Between British folly and Indian frustration, the Allied cause, particularly the futures of the hard-pressed Chinese and Russians, trembled in the balance. In the aftermath of the unsuccessful Cripps Mission, Gandhi's decision to launch a mass struggle created a further painful dilemma for Nehru. Gandhi's idea of initiating civil disobedience when the Japanese were on India's doorstep at first seemed fantastic to Nehru. His mind was full of thoughts of citizen armies, home guards and guerrilla warfare to beat off the Japanese invaders. Deep heart-searching and anguish led him to the point of considering deviation from the Congress policy towards the war. It was with some difficulty that he was persuaded not to cooperate with the Allies.[31]

Eventually, Nehru conformed to Gandhi's "Quit India" stand even though he was conscious that it "gave second place to logic and reason" and "was not a politician's approach but that of a people desperate and reckless of consequences."[32] Before he did so, he had persuaded Gandhi to agree that Allied troops would remain on Indian soil during the war, and the provisional government of free India would throw all its resources into the struggle against Fascism. For Gandhi with his passionate commitment to nonviolence, this was a painful agreement. Nehru's decision to support the Mahatma in the "Quit India" movement was thus not really as one-sided a compromise as some of his critics said.

"Godly power of the Mahatma," wrote M. N. Roy, "has over-powered the human wish of the romantic politician [Nehru] . . . for throughout his whole career he has blindly followed Mr. Gandhi. In fact he has no independence of thought or action."[33] What M. N. Roy failed to see was that in reaching a compromise Nehru did not make all the concessions. If the internationalist had given in to the nationalist in Nehru, the pacifist had given in to the patriot in Gandhi.

After spending nearly three years in jail, Nehru was released in June 1945 just before the Simla Conference. Here began tri-angular negotiations between the British Government, the Congress and the Muslim League which culminated in the transfer of power and the partition of India two years later. In these negotia-tions, Nehru, Vallabhbhai Patel, and Abul Kalam Azad played leading parts, but they remained in touch with Gandhi and took his advice. Only in the last phase of the negotiations, toward the end of 1946 and the beginning of 1947, when Gandhi was tour-ing the riot-torn countryside of East Bengal and Bihar, did his influence on events become minimal. This may have been due partly to his absence from Delhi—the hub of political activity —and partly to the swiftness with which the political landscape changed during this period owing to the eagerness of the Muslim League to benefit from the British decision to quit India and the anxiety of the Congress for a speedy and smooth transfer of power. In the aftermath of the Muslim League's Direct Action Day at Calcutta in August 1946, communal violence spread like a prairie fire and threatened to engulf the whole country. At the center the conflict between Congress and Muslim League members paralyzed the Interim Government. As the danger of a civil war loomed on the horizon, Nehru, Patel, and most Congress leaders came to the painful conclusion that the partition of the country would be less of an evil than a forced and fragile union. They decided to salvage three-fourths of India from the chaos that threatened the whole. Against this background the Congress Working Committee discussed the partition of the provinces of the Punjab and Bengal in March 1947 and accepted the Mount-batten Plan for the transfer of power and the partition of the country as its corollary in June. The final decision was taken against Gandhi's advice.

Michael Brecher has suggested that Nehru and Patel opted for the partition of the country because they were tempted by "the prize of power."[34] Human motives are rarely unmixed, but in the summer of 1947 partition seemed the lesser evil not only to Nehru and Patel, but to the entire Congress leadership with a few exceptions such as those of Abdul Ghaffar Khan and Jayaprakash Narayan. Gandhi's eleventh hour proposal that the Viceroy call upon Jinnah to form an exclusively Muslim League Government was a bold gesture, but the Congress leaders, after their ex-perience of association with Muslim League ministers in the In-terim Government, were in no mood to endorse it. Nor did Gandhi's alternative of a mass struggle appeal to them. Struggle against whom? The British were in any case going, and the Mus-lim League with its calculated mixture of bluster and bullying was hardly susceptible to the moral nuances of satyagraha. J. B. Kri-palani explained his predicament: "Today also I feel that he [Gandhi] by his supreme fearlessness is correct and my stand is defective. Why then am I not with him? It is because I feel that he has as yet found no way of tackling the [Hindu-Muslim] pro-blem on a mass basis."[35]

To Nehru and Patel it seemed that the Mahatma's idealism had outrun the needs of a critical and developing crisis, that the intransigence of the Muslim League and the mounting chaos in the country really left no alternative to partition, that insistence on unity under such circumstances was to court even greater dis-aster. Gandhi's colleagues admired his faith in nonviolence, but most of them believed that he was an uncompromising prophet rather than a practical statesman. Gandhi had been isolated be-fore. In 1940, the Congress had declined to accept nonviolence as a shield against external danger. Seven years later, the party refused to embrace ahimsa as a shield against internal disorder.

Gandhi seems to have had a lingering regret that in the final stage of the negotiations with the British Government Nehru and Patel had bypassed him. Nevertheless, he lent them his powerful support at the crucial meetings of the Working Committee and the All India Congress Committee. During the five and a half months which remained to him, he wore himself out in an effort to heal the wounds inflicted by the partition and became, in the words of Lord Mountbatten, a "one-man boundary force."

Gandhi was not the man to nurse a grievance, and there is no evidence to show that the events leading to the partition created any permanent estrangement between him and Nehru. As Prime Minister, Nehru continued to lean on Gandhi for advice and moral support during the latter half of 1947. A reminder of this dependence came to Nehru within a few hours of the tragedy on January 30, 1948. "I was sitting in my chair . . . worried about Bapu's funeral. The colossal problem that it presented baffled me. Suddenly I said to myself: 'Let me go and consult Bapu.' "[36]

Gandhi's death sublimated Nehru's relationship with him. The heroic fight of the Mahatma against fanaticism and violence in his last months, and finally his martyrdom, burned themselves into Nehru's soul. The memory of "the Master," as Nehru loved to recall him, suffused with a fresh glow and nourished by mingled feelings of love, gratitude, and guilt, remained with him till the last. He told a correspondent in 1957 that he could not write at length on Gandhi as "I get emotionally worked up and that is no mood to write. If I was a poet, which I am not, perhaps that mood might help."[37] The awesome responsibility of running the party and the government perhaps gave him a fresh, retrospective insight into the methods of the Mahatma who had carried the burden of conducting the movement for nearly thirty years. During Gandhi's lifetime, he and Nehru both made compromises reflecting each other's point of view. The sharp criticisms of Gandhi's philosophy which appeared in Nehru's *Autobiography* were greatly toned down in *Discovery of India,* published a decade later. During these years, Nehru went a long way toward rediscovering both India and Gandhi.

The political equation between Gandhi and Nehru, which extended over a quarter of a century, was not static. It continually evolved and sought a new equilibrium in response not only to the inner drives of two men of exceptional energy and integrity, but also to the realities of the changing political scene in India. During the first ten years, the partnership was really between Gandhi and Motilal. Young Nehru's role was that of a favorite and earnest disciple of the Mahatma. The Lahore Congress brought Jawaharlal to the forefront of national politics, but not until the late 1930's did he become a factor in the party. It is an index of his rising political stature that his dissent was merely an inconvenience to the Congress Establishment in the 1920's, but in 1936, it brought the party to the verge of a split. He owed his position in the party and the country in a great measure to his own qualities: his high idealism and dynamism, tireless energy and robust optimism, infectious faith in the destiny of his party and his country, his glamour for youth and charisma for the masses. Nevertheless, it is doubtful that he could have reached the apex of the party leadership so early and so decisively if Gandhi had not catapulted him into it at critical junctures in 1929 and 1936.

Gandhi knew that Jawaharlal was not a blind follower and that he had a mind of his own. Their philosophies of life diverged widely, but they were at one in their desire to rid the country of foreign rule and of gross poverty and social and economic inequalities. Gandhi wanted to harness Nehru's great talents and energies, and he was confident that he could contain the impetuous and rebellious spirit of his younger friend. On the eve of the 1936 crisis in the party, the Mahatma assured an English correspondent: "But though Jawaharlal is extreme in his presentation of his methods, he is sober in action. So far as I know him, he will not precipitate a conflict. . . . My own feeling is that Jawaharlal will accept the decision of the majority of his colleagues."[38]

Why did two men of such diverse background and temperament work together? The simple answer is that they needed each other. In 1919, young Nehru needed Gandhi to provide an outlet for his passionate nationalism, and Gandhi, about to enter the Indian political stage, needed able lieutenants. He had already enlisted Mahadev Desai, Vallabhbhai Patel and Rajendra Prasad. It is not surprising that young Jawaharlal should have caught the Mahatma's perceptive eye and evoked from the outset a special consideration. Jawaharlal was to become Gandhi's link with the young generation and his window on the world. Informed by study and travel, he became Gandhi's mentor on international affairs. His passion for clarity and logic often clashed with the Mahatma's intuitive and pragmatic approach. But he discovered before long that the Mahatma had an uncanny sense of the mood of the Indian masses, their potential and their limitations, and that his political decisions were in fact sounder than the explanations with which he clothed them. Nehru realized the indispensability of Gandhi's leadership and, therefore, never pressed his differences to an open breach with him. Whatever his inner doubts about the potential of nonviolence for changing the hearts of those who wielded political and economic power, Jawaharlal felt certain that Gandhi was leading the country in the right direction. Indeed, realizing Gandhi's receptivity, flexibility, and unpredictability, Nehru continued to hope that eventually the Mahatma's weight would be thrown in favor of radicalizing India's politics and economy.

Gandhi's link with Jawaharlal Nehru transcended the political nexus. His extraordinary capacity to love and be loved was experienced by many of his colleagues and their families. But for the Nehru family he seems to have had a special corner in his heart. With Motilal his relationship was that of a colleague rather than that of a mentor. Jawaharlal was doubtless a disciple but a favorite one. The Mahatma's face shone with pleasure and pride in the company of young Nehru whom he hailed as his son long before he described him as his heir. Intellectual and political differences did not diminish Gandhi's affection which was deeply reciprocated by Jawaharlal. There was hardly a major domestic decision—whether it was the treatment of his ailing wife, the education of his daughter, or the marriage of his sister —on which Jawaharlal did not seek the Mahatma's advice and blessing. It was to "Bapu" that the family instinctively turned for solace in moments of grief. When Kamala Nehru was dying in Switzerland, Jawaharlal cabled her condition daily not only to her mother in India but to Gandhi as well.

Gandhi had much less difficulty in understanding Nehru than Nehru had in understanding Gandhi. The Mahatma seems to have sensed almost immediately, and more clearly than Motilal, the deep loneliness, idealism and restless energy of young Nehru. Indeed in the earlier years, Gandhi acted as a bridge between father and son. For Gandhi, the crucial test came when, after his visit to Europe in 1927, Jawaharlal suddenly seemed to have outgrown the political and economic framework of the party. Gandhi's reaction to young Nehru's rebellion was characteristic. He did not attempt to muzzle him. On the contrary, he encouraged him to be candid about their differences. "I suggest a dignified way of unfurling your banner. Write to me a letter for publication showing your differences. I will print it in *Young India* and write a brief reply."[39] Subsequently when Jawaharlal was straining at the leash after signing the Delhi Manifesto, Gandhi wrote him: "Let this incident be a lesson. Resist me always when my suggestion does not appeal to your head or heart. I shall not love you the less for that resistance."[40]

Gandhi's refusal to impose his ideas on Nehru could not but have had a moderating influence on Jawaharlal. The lack of resistance from the Mahatma reduced the incentive for an open revolt. Repeatedly Gandhi offered to step off the political stage altogether and to leave the field to Nehru and others. Since Gandhi did not owe his influence in the party to any office, he was not vulnerable; it was pointless to seek to overthrow a leader who was always willing to retire voluntarily.

Nehru reconciled the conflict between his mind and heart,

between his own convictions and loyalty to Gandhi and the party, through inner struggle and anguish. Nobody knew more than Nehru how much he owed to Gandhi. From the Mahatma he imbibed an ethical framework, a concern for the "naked hungry mass" of India, and faith in peaceful and patient methods.

The working partnership between Nehru and Gandhi lasted until the end, but their philosophies of life never really converged. In October 1945, a few months before the negotiations for the final demission of British power began, Gandhi wrote to Nehru: "I am now an old man. . . . I have, therefore, named you as my heir. I must, however, understand my heir and my heir should understand me. Then alone shall I be content."[41] The Mahatma went on to express his conviction that truth and non-violence could be realized only in the simplicity of village life and in the organization of free India as a federation of self-reliant village republics. Nehru replied:

> The question before us is not one of truth versus untruth or non-violence versus violence. One assumes as one must, that true cooperation and peaceful methods must be aimed at and a society which encourages these must be our objective. The whole question is how to achieve this society and what its content should be. I do not understand why a village should necessarily embody truth and non-violence. A village, normally speaking, is backward intellectually and culturally and no progress can be made from a backward environment. Narrow-minded people are much more likely to be untruthful and violent. . . .[42]

The argument between Gandhi and Nehru in 1945 on what constituted the good society remained inconclusive, but Nehru adhered to the line he had always taken in public and private. "We cannot stop the river of change," he had written in his autobiography, "or cut ourselves adrift from it and psychologically, we who have eaten the apple of Eden cannot forget the taste and go back to primitiveness."[43] Hardly any one affected surprise when in Gandhi's lifetime the Constituent Assembly set itself to the task of framing a constitution for a strong nation-state based on parliamentary democracy, with all the paraphernalia of a civil service, army, navy and air force, along with an infrastructure for modern industry. For Nehru and his colleagues, the question in 1947, as a shrewd critic has recently pointed out, was not that of personal loyalty to Gandhi, but "a matter of social perspective and principles"—a choice between "a strong industrial (and military) state versus a commonwealth of barely self-sufficient agricultural communities."[44] Nehru chose the first as, indeed, he had said in the Mahatma's lifetime that he would.

Nehru would have been the last person to profess that he was following Gandhi's blueprint for an independent India during his years in power. Even if it had been possible to recognize such a blueprint, the vision could not have been adapted to the mechanism of the modern state. *Sarvodaya,* unlike socialism, cannot be legislated into existence. The changes it postulates in the minds and hearts of men can be better attempted through voluntary efforts and the example of devoted men rather than through the authority of parliaments, cabinets, civil services, courts and the police. In fairness to Nehru, it must be acknowledged that he applied Gandhiism as far as he could to the needs of a modern nation-state. The spirit of Gandhi may be seen in Nehru's consistent respect for individual liberty and secularism, his rejection of violence and regimentation, and his determination to find a national consensus within the parliamentary system. Like Gandhi, he had a deep concern for the small peasant, the landless laborer, and the industrial worker. The concept of Five Year Plans, though far removed from Gandhian economics, stressed the uplift of rural India and included programs for community development, village self-government and cottage industries.

In foreign policy Nehru was not Gandhian enough to advocate unilateral disarmament of India nor did he turn the other cheek to Pakistan and China. Nevertheless, throughout his years in office, he threw his weight in favor of nonalignment with military blocs, conciliation and peaceful negotiation of differences between nations and the widening of the area of peace. The deep conviction with which he pursued these aims, despite difficulties and rebuffs, doubtless stemmed from his long association with Gandhi. During his twilight years, in a world darkened by growing cynicism, violence and ruthlessness, Nehru was speaking more and more in Gandhian accents, pleading for the linking of the "scientific approach" and the "spiritualistic approach"[45] and warning the Planning Commission against the dangers of "giganticism."[46] Almost the last thing he wrote pointed out that while progress in science, technology, and production were desirable, "we must not forget that the essential objective to be aimed at is the quality of the individual and the concept of *Dharma* underlying it."[47]

NOTES

1. Percival Spear, "Nehru," *Modern Asian Studies* I (January 1967):18.
2. M. N. Roy, "Jawaharlal Nehru: An Enigma or a Tragedy?" in *Jawaharlal Nehru, A Critical Tribute,* ed. A. B. Shah (Bombay: Manaktalas, 1965), p. 39.
3. Hiren Mukerjee, *The Gentle Colossus: A Study of Jawaharlal Nehru* (Calcutta: Manisha Granthalaya Private, 1964), pp. 71-75.
4. B. R. Nanda, *The Nehrus, Motilal and Jawaharlal* (London: Allen & Unwin, 1962), pp. 170-71.
5. Tibor Mende, *Conversations with Mr. Nehru* (London: Secker & Warburg, 1956), p. 23.
6. *Ibid.,* pp. 24-31.
7. Letter, Jawaharlal Nehru to G. A. Lambert, Chief Secretary,

Government of United Provinces, July 4, 1921, Nehru
Papers.

8. Jawaharlal Nehru, *An Autobiography* (London: The Bodley Head, 1942), p. 77.

9. Letter, Gandhi to Jawaharlal Nehru, January 4, 1928,
Nehru Papers.

10. Letter, Gandhi to Motilal, March 3, 1928, Nehru Papers.

11. Quoted in Pyarelal, "Gandhi-Nehru: A Unique Relationship," *Link,* 7 (May 30, 1965), 32.

12. Nehru, *An Autobiography,* p. 194.

13. *Ibid.,* pp. 257-59. Gandhi told Lord Irwin (Halifax) that
Jawaharlal had wept on his shoulder, "over this tragedy of
the betrayal of India." See *Talking of Gandhiji,* ed. Francis
Watson (Bombay: Orient Longmans, 1957), p. 63.

14. Nehru, *An Autobiography,* p. 490.

15. Letter, Jawaharlal Nehru to Gandhi, August 13, 1934,
Nehru Papers.

16. J. B. Kripalani, *Indian National Congress* (Bombay: Vora
& Co., 1946), p. 12.

17. Narendra Deva, *Socialism and the National Revolution*
(Bombay: Padma Publications Ltd., 1946), pp. 28-29.

18. Telegram, Government of India to the Secretary of State
for India, October 24, 1933. Home Political Confidential F.
31 of 1933, National Archives of India.

19. Note dated March 16, 1938 by Jawaharlal Nehru, recorded
at Khali. Nehru Papers.

20. Nehru, *An Autobiography,* p. 515.

21. Letter, Jawaharlal Nehru to Sri Prakasa, May 3, 1936, Sri
Prakasa Collection.

22. Letter, Jawaharlal Nehru to Syed Mahmud, May 5, 1936,
Dr. Syed Mahmud Collection.

23. *News Chronicle,* November 12, 1936.

24. Letter, Jawaharlal Nehru to Subhas Bose, February 4, 1939,
Nehru Papers.

25. *Ibid.,* April 3, 1939.

26. Letter, Gandhi to Jawaharlal Nehru, July 15, 1936, Nehru
Papers.

27. Mukerjee, *Gentle Colossus,* p. 71.

28. E. M. S. Namboodiripad, *The Mahatma and the Ism* (New Delhi: People's Publishing House, 1958), pp. 74-75.

29. Letter, Rafi Ahmed Kidwai to Jawaharlal Nehru, undated, Nehru Papers.

30. Letter, Gandhi to Jawaharlal Nehru, October 26, 1939, Nehru Papers.

31. Abul Kalam Azad, *India Wins Freedom* (Bombay: Orient Longmans, 1959), p. 65.

32. Jawaharlal Nehru, *Discovery of India,* 6th ed. (Calcutta: Signet Press, 1956), pp. 504-55.

33. Quoted in *Dawn,* June 28, 1942.

34. Michael Brecher, *Nehru: A Political Biography* (London: Oxford University Press, 1959), p. 379.

35. *Congress Bulletin,* No. 4, July 10, 1947, p. 9.

36. Quoted in Pyarelal, "Gandhi-Nehru," p. 32.

37. Quoted in Mukerjee, *Gentle Colossus,* p. 31.

38. Letter, Gandhi to Agatha Harrison, April 30, 1936, Nehru Papers.

39. Letter, Gandhi to Jawaharlal Nehru, January 17, 1928, Nehru Papers.

40. Letter, Gandhi to Jawaharlal Nehru, November 4, 1929, Nehru Papers.

41. Quoted in Pyarelal, *Towards New Horizons* (Ahmedabad: Navajivan Publishing House, 1959), p. 4.

42. *Ibid.,* p. 5.

43. Nehru, *An Autobiography,* p. 511.

44. P. H. Patwardhan in N. K. Bose and P. H. Patwardhan, *Gandhi in Indian Politics* (Bombay: Lalvani Publishing House, 1967), p. 85.

45. *Statesman,* December 1, 1958.

46. Quoted in Shriman Narayan, *Letters from Gandhi, Nehru, Vinoba* (Bombay: Asia Publishing House, 1968), p. 10.

47. Foreword by Nehru to Narayan, *Letters.*

2

GANDHI'S LIEUTENANTS—
VARIETIES OF FOLLOWERSHIP

Susanne Hoeber Rudolph

The analysis of leaders cannot rest content with the enumeration of their attributes and capabilities nor can these attributes be understood by regarding the leader as an isolate. Relations to others constitute his meaning. To grasp those relations requires a follower-oriented approach that attends to the qualities and interests of a leader's constituents and the articulation of those qualities and interests with the leader's style and appeal. But there is never one following. There are many, at graded degrees of intimacy and relation to the leader, and they bring to the relationship with him the requirements of various psyches, roles, and social and political interests.

While a follower-oriented approach to the analysis and understanding of leadership may be fruitful in any study of leadership, it is of special interest in relation to Gandhi. Unlike a more rigorously ideological leader, who might expect the human material with which he deals to adapt itself rather precisely to his movement's normative and behavioral requirements, Gandhi was strongly attuned to the varying inner states and potentialities of his followers. A movement leader committed to shaping men, he suited the shaping to the characterological contours of his followers, sensitive to the limits of their adaptability. This was not invariably true. His sensitivity failed him with his sons and wife, whom he sought to mold beyond their tolerance, and with some significant public figures such as Jinnah and Ambedkar. Nonetheless, it was a distinguishing mark of his leadership.

His capacity to serve the variety of strengths and needs of those close to him and his skill and versatility in shaping his response to each had less relevance for Gandhi's mass following than it did for his religious followers, especially the dwellers in the ashrams, the religious retreats that institutionalized his spiritual teaching and leadership. The co-leaders who joined the nationalist movement in response to Gandhi's revitalization of it were also affected by his sensitivity. Much of his success in amplifying himself to wider audiences in India lay in the psychological and stylistic versatility of which he was capable, i.e., his ability to be the Mahatma, Bapu, and Gandhi.[1] What follows is an exploration of this versatility with reference to two types of followers, his mass following and the ashramites.

The mass following constitutes an amorphous category which can be given precision by a number of approaches. One can reach the mass following by situational analysis, asking who became involved, in what capacities, at leading moments— Khaira, Bardoli, the Dandi Salt March, the Rowlatt Satyagraha —using the perspectives and methods of crowd research associated with the work of George Rudé. Donald W. Ferrell has given us an instance of situational analysis which shows, for example, the structure of the Rowlatt agitation in Delhi city in 1919.[2] He outlines a complex structure of leadership and participation extending from the well-known national leadership of the Home Rule League to the less-known Delhi notables, especially of the commercial and professional classes, such as Rai Sahib Pearey Lal, vice-president of the municipal committee and president of the Delhi bar association. Secondary echelons of leadership, such as K. A. Desai, a Gujarati immigrant to the city and manager of the Birla cotton mill in Delhi, and Abdul Said, Maulvi and teacher at Madrassa Aminia, were participants. There were journalists and editors of various Muslim and Hindu papers as well as Muslim divines who led the Hindu and Muslim artisans in the movement. Swami Shradhanand, the Arya Samaj leader, took part in the agitation.

One can also specify a mass following through organizational analysis, asking who participated in what ways in the committee structures built by the nationalist movement, using the perspectives of students of party, or of studies of non-party political organizations, such as Crane Brinton's work on the Jacobins or Eugene Black's on associations in eighteenth-century English politics. An instance of such organizational analysis in the Indian context is Anil Bhatt's study of the social groupings of the Patidars in Bardoli district. They began in the early 1900's to build multi-functional structures out of caste materials.[3] Bhatt's study reveals the organizational base which Sardar Patel and Gandhi used in connection with the Bardoli Satyagraha. Neither the situational nor organizational analysis, however, yields data or insights about psychological and symbolic questions of followership and needs and styles.

Here I want to draw attention to less structured and less sophisticated rural and small town crowds that responded directly to Gandhi's presence, activities and reputation. A major part of his travel programs involved exposure to such people. The meetings along the way provided an intense crowd setting for the participants; they represented endurance tests for Gandhi and his entourage. While they sometimes involved speaking, they more often required him merely to show himself to those who had come to see. Thus, Krishnadas:

> And so when nearing Sasaram, we saw that the whole of the town had come out, and were standing in a double line, some two or three miles long. . . . Our car had to stop; but that very instant, the whole crowd from every side closed upon us. The pressure was so great that although we were inside the car, we felt we were almost out of breath. As we were some seven or eight in the car, these people were hard put to it to discover which of us must be Mahatma Gandhi; and in their

perplexity some would be fighting to clutch at the feet of Kripalani, some to clutch at the feet of Ram Binode;—while others would feel themselves blest to have merely touched my person. And so group after group came as in a regular stream; nor did they leave us until in the manner aforesaid they had had a look of us and a touch of our body. This simple faith of the people touched, indeed, the deepest chords of one's heart. But . . . to us this manifestation of love partook of the nature of love's tyranny and seemed to be past endurance.[4]

Such mass confrontations have everywhere become the fate of leading figures in the democratic era. But the Gandhian experience has features that distinguish it from others. While Gandhi was travelling by train from Karachi, we are told by Chandiwala:

Cooked food, fruit, and milk were brought to us in such an abundance that we were literally buried in it. Crowds would ask for Bapu's *prasad* [sanctified food that has been offered to a diety and subsequently distributed to the worshippers] and though we kept distributing everything we received, still there was no end to it.[5]

In inquiring what meanings Gandhi had for these crowds, one is tempted to characterize the relationship in terms suggested by Freudian or pre-Freudian psychology, the older psychological theory of crowds. One envisions a kind of magic moment of psychic fusion between a leader's exhortation and the followers' rising level of enthusiasm, a moment characterized by an abstract ecstatic intimacy which has its counterpart in American fundamentalist conversionary religions. Since we do not know in any detail what the inner feelings were of those who participated in these rituals of intimacy, such a view of the matter must remain a matter of speculation. On the other hand, there is a less inward, more routinized alternative which may explain these events. As against, or beside, the idea of psychic fusion one may evoke the efficacy attributed to magic or sacred objects and persons which has a considerable cultural tradition in the Indian setting as in others. The word darshan in Indian culture implies that a worshipper believes that viewing a deity, or a saintly man, is an auspicious experience, one which brings religious merit and perhaps personal good fortune. It is related to those ideas in Western Christianity which inspire pilgrimages to sacred sites and sacred relics. People came to have darshan of Gandhi; his personal reputation for saintliness, his political importance and influence and his status as a celebrity all seem to have played a part in giving personal exposure to him a semi-religious qualtiy.

Gandhi's peripatetic style is also not unprecedented. It has its counterpart in the journeys of the saintly bhakti teachers of the devotional faiths who sang their songs and preached in large and small centers throughout India. They were a part of the oral tradition and taught through it. Gandhi used their songs in his prayer meetings, notably the songs of the Vaishnavite saints with their egalitarian and devotional themes. His public came to hear both a political leader and a spiritual guide.

Thus his relationship to his mass followers represents one type of followership and a form of communication appropriate to it. It is a relationship in which Gandhi appears as a generalized sacred presence as a result of his reputation for saintly conduct. Its intense impersonality establishes no specific two-way bond between Gandhi and his constituents except the abstract bond which the follower may conjure up out of psychic and symbolic materials within himself.

Gandhi's response to an enthusiastic, transcendent, "fused" audience, however, was the reverse of what might be expected. Instead of heightening their enthusiasm or using it as a means toward ecstatic commitment, he usually attempted to lower the psychic temperature by his matter of fact, even low-key, style. He opposed the tendency of a group to become a mass, emphasizing, instead, its component persons by setting tasks that had to be accomplished at a given moment by individuals. During the

Calcutta riots, for example, Gandhi asked each Hindu to find
and help one Muslim. He wanted responsible persons, not an
enthusiastic crowd.

Gandhi communicated quite differently, much less ab-
stractly, with the ashramites, men and women, who sought the
discipline, order, and authority that a quasi-monastic setting provides. That discipline, to be sure, was neo-traditional at best. It
bore the mark of Gandhi's coeducational modifications which
were not the norm in traditional ashram arrangements. It was
modified further by Gandhi's industrious, Ruskinesque and
banya overlay to older, less busy versions of an ashram. Nationalist ashram members provided the disciplined cadres for the
movement, although political action was often less a political
than a religious self-realization. The political goal provided much
of the élan for a more traditional self-transcendence, as it did for
the militant ascetics in the forest ashram of Bankim Chandra's
Anandamath.

While much has been said rhetorically about the fact that
Gandhi had both a political and a religious dimension, the consequences of the second dimension for his personal "job descrip-
tion" have not been taken sufficiently seriously. To be "abbot"
and spiritual director for some two hundred ashramites would
have been a full-time task, and Gandhi took the responsibility
very seriously. The intensity of religious vocation among the
ashramites differed, and others, such as Vinoba Bhave or Shri
Kedarnath, shared the work of religious inquiry and guidance
with Gandhi. Vinoba provided an alternative position and discipline, less worldly and more traditional than Gandhi's industrious and service-oriented variant of asceticism. But most of the
ashramites felt, when a relationship worked, that Gandhi knew
them personally and that he grasped and appreciated their individual psychic and religious needs. They accepted him as a
personal moral teacher on the model of the conventional guru-
chela relationship. Such a relationship is capable of multiple

psychic variations, more and less distant. It must often have existed in routinized form, drained of affect. For some, though, the experience involved intense personal attachment that arose from strong psychic transference on the part of the disciple. The bhakti tradition again suggests an analogy for the tone of these relationships. The devotional faiths, distinguishable by their sensitivity to emotional tone from the more abstract, routinized Brahmanic quest for self-transformation through knowledge and asceticism, encouraged strongly affective relationships to God and to those who are guides to God. They emphasized the love of God, fusion with God, and intense concentration on God. The path might lie in the faithful obedience to the guru who falls psychic heir to the love, devotion and concentration that is directed through him towards God. The worship of the guru's feet, important symbolic ritual for the bhakta, symbolizes the pure-hearted self-submission which plays a role in bhakti as it does in aspects of Christian doctrine. Their doctrines may also emphasize an utter yielding up of the self, a giving over of all remnants of self not only to God but to him who is a guide to God. In such a scheme, unwillingness to yield up oneself is a sign of failure in the quest. Insofar as such doctrines might designate resistance to a guru's direction as signs of spiritual imperfection, they place a great burden of self-insight and human integrity on the guide. Gurus do not, like psychiatrists, receive systematic training to help them distinguish when a patient is resisting analysis and when it is the psychiatrist's *hubris* that makes him call a legitimate ego assertion "resistance." Gandhi's role for some of the ashramites can be understood by reference to these different traditions.

Vinoba Bhave, who had the strongest religious vocation among those who followed Gandhi, has written about the kind of presence Gandhi was to such followers. Great men, he says, can be likened to "the motherly cow. The cow feeds the calf on its milk with the result the calf grows from day to day."[6] To a Western ear, that part of Vinoba's image which evokes calf-like dependency, sounds most loudly; yet growth is the other, less striking, part of the image. Both features figure in Gandhi's relationships to the ashramites.

The autobiographical recalls of followers who became ashramites suggest the theme of pure-hearted submission. It was the first moment or two of encounter with Gandhi which imprinted the style which would subsequently characterize much of the relationship. One such follower was Brij Krishna Chandiwala, the son of a wealthy Delhi commercial family. He first encountered Gandhi during the Rowlatt Satyagraha:

> During his country-wide tour, he came to Delhi where a mass meeting to protest against the bill was organized at Pahterwala grounds. It was the first meeting I attended where I heard Gandhiji speak. I was standing near the platform in the corner, when I had an intense desire to touch his feet. I saw him advancing toward the platform. Gathering together my courage, I rushed towards him, touched his holy feet, and put the dust on my forehead.[7]

The account is paralleled by that of Balvant Sinha, a former soldier and one of the more prickly and difficult ashramites. Chandiwala calls his book *At the Feet of Bapu*; Sinha, with a slightly less intense submission, uses the title, *Under the Shelter of Bapu.*

It was their wish for spiritual and psychic guidance which placed such men with Gandhi. His correspondence and other dealings with them suggest that he brought a great capacity for intimacy to his roles as abbot and spiritual director of souls in the ashram. He also used his guidance to make men who often hoped to evade management of their own fates by placing themselves under his care less reliant on him and his strength. While he was sufficiently present to provide them sustenance, he sought to release them from the need for it.

In these two relationships, then, to crowds and to the

ashramites, Gandhi offered two different aspects of himself. Before crowds, what was required of him was his presence, to which quasi-magical potency was attributed. The degree of unquestioned obeisance which his presence evoked fluctuated with historical events. During periods of Hindu-Muslim tension, he did not receive the unreserved devotion of crowds from either community. Their obeisance did not usually depend on any specific words or acts of his or on any interactions initiated by him. It was no more necessary that he should respond in these settings than that a temple deity, carried in procession, should do so. The devotion or attention afforded him depended on his past reputation for political and spiritual efficacy. His relations to the ashramites, on the other hand, were quite different. Here a great deal was demanded of him in the way of psychic sympathy with various souls engaged in a variety of secular and trans-secular quests. While one role required endurance, the other required moral and psychic versatility and insight. Both had in common a strong analogy to the bhakti tradition, to its practice of peripatetic teaching and its requirement of personal devotion to a guru.

These relationships raise more general questions about the type of psychological authority Gandhi exercised. If we begin with the assumption that psychological symmetry is the norm for human relationships among adult males, an assumption marked among Western observers, the asymmetrical features in Gandhi's leadership become problematic. To take the extreme case of Arthur Koestler, who can be relied upon to invalidate a plausible case by overstatement:

> As long as Gandhi remained the Bapu, the men around him, including Nehru, were virtually incapable of going against his decisions, even when these struck them as illogical and dangerous—as they quite often did.[8]

But similar Indian remarks are not wanting, notably among more Westernized Indians. Nehru writes: "And can anything be greater coercion than the psychic coercion of Gandhiji which reduces many of his intimate followers and colleagues to a state of mental pulp?"[9]

There is some basis for such a view. Gandhi's relationships with the ashramites were evidently asymmetrical, a fact that is related, on the one hand, to the culturally defined role expectations between spiritual directors and their pupils in India (and elsewhere?) and, on the other, to the psychic needs of the ashramites.[10] The two are presumably related: the roles must have seemed inviting to those who wished to "worship the feet" of the guru. But what about Gandhi's own psychological requirements? We must assume that cultural and psychic attributes enabled him, at least, to bear such asymmetry; at most, to welcome it. The larger question is, were asymmetrical relationships the only ones of which he was capable?

It is hazardous to assume that psychological generalizations that formulate a man's relationship in one context necessarily fit another, i.e., that Gandhi's relationships to the ashramites or to his family provide a necessary paradigm for other relationships. Some men may indeed possess a pattern of psychic possibilities so narrow as to suggest that either ideological or psychological limits or both have barred them from perceiving and responding to psychological or role variations among followers. Strongly ideological leadership, leadership which relies on coercion, or leadership which is willing to restrict lieutenants to personality types drawn from a very narrow spectrum of psychological make-ups, may succeed with a minimum of psychic versatility. In Gandhi's case, it becomes apparent that providing sustenance to questing souls that needed a guide did not exhaust his psychological capacities. His strong concern to make them walk alone already suggests that he did not "need" them at his feet. But the wider range, as well as the ultimate limits, of his psychic versatility can best be illustrated by examining relationships in which there was less cultural presumption of asymmetry than existed in the ashram. Such relationships were those which obtained with the co-leaders of the nationalist movement.

A number of considerations will guide me in analyzing Gandhi's relations to these men. A leader's capacity to generate and hold an immediate circle of followers attached to him by face-to-face intercourse is related to both his and the follower's psycho-social development. Hence we must have regard for the nature of the follower's attachments to others that have presumed to direct him, notably parents or, in India, an elder brother. The fit of this psycho-history with the follower's relationship to his leader must be noted.

Different followership styles are available in different so-cieties. Followership has a much more hierarchical meaning in the Indian context than it has, for example, in many American political and private associations. In both societies, however, re-lationships are apt to be differentiated by roles and psychological idiosyncrasy. The class, caste, ritual, occupational and age settings of leaders and followers as well as their psychological propensities create variation. The contrasting followership styles characterizing John F. Kennedy and his Boston-mayor grandfather suggest class and subculture play a part even in the same family if it is mobile over several generations. A moment's reflection on Lyndon B. Johnson and Eugene McCarthy suggests that varying psycho-logical needs or tolerances invite different styles of discipleship. To investigate followership, then, requires attention to one di-mension that is affected by the psychological autobiography of leader and follower and to another that is affected by the cultural definitions of leader-follower relations. The cultural dimension is in turn heterogeneous, because each society provides alternative styles of followership. It is within this range of possibilities that a leader exercises his specific genius and within which he en-counters his limitations.

To specify the ingredients of the psycho-cultural approach to followership is easier than to carry it through. In the case of Gandhi's followers and others, early life-history material is often lacking altogether or, in any case, lacking in depth. Despite the influence of psycho-analytic perspectives, childhood continues to be considered childish and many of its most significant episodes irrelevant for the man that was the child. This is both more and less true of Indian biographical material. Psychological insight rarely sharpens the narrator's perception. At the same time, conventions of reserve frequent in Western biography are sometimes less observed. We have, for example, a clear view of Nehru's youth due to Motilal and Jawaharlal's precocious correspondence and to B. R. Nanda's sensitive biographical work.[11]

I would like, eventually, to examine Gandhi's relations with four co-leaders of substantial national importance who were very close to him but who were also quite different from each other. The four are: Jamnalal Bajaj, treasurer of the Indian National Congress and States Peoples Freedom Movement leader; Vallabhbhai Patel, member of the Congress Working Committee and Deputy Prime Minister of India from 1947 to 1950, when he died; G. D. Birla, financier of Congress; and Jawaharlal Nehru, Indian National Congress President and Prime Minister of India from 1947 until his death in 1964. All four, except Bajaj, differed from the ashramites in that they entered the relationship with Gandhi from more independent political and psychic bases and without the strongly asymmetrical assumptions of spiritual guide and follower. None of them, again except Bajaj, was of those who worship the feet of the guru. Rather, they were peers, building on Gandhi's inspiration, innovating within the movement he led and shaped, bringing to it important perspectives and followings. The surrender of self which was the significant element in the ashram relations was replaced by a greater reservation of self. Indeed, it was their marginal or substantial differences from Gandhi, their separate rather than merged identities, that made them important to him. He amplified himself and his leadership through their diversity.

His relationship to these followers was often in a state of tension between attachment and dissent. There was that in Gandhi that made separating from or adhering to him a more intense matter than diverging from a less relentless man. His psychology had in common with that of religious and political ideologues the feeling that no view was ever a matter of indifference. Every position had meaning and required examination and defense. He diverged from other ideologues in that he resisted dispensing with those who differed and did not restrict his following to those who would suffer his relentlessness unresisting. It is characteristic of his relations with co-leaders that they were often not with him in fundamental matters. Yet they adhered even when the differences between them were basic. Patel, Birla, and Nehru in their recollections of him stress the differences between themselves and him. Thus Birla, after a passage in which he declares himself Gandhi's devotee, adds hastily:

> It would be totally incorrect, however, to say that I agreed with Gandhiji on all points. In fact, on most problems I took my own independent counsel. There was not much in common between us so far as our mode of life went. Gandhiji was a saintly person who had renounced all comforts and luxuries of life . . . he believed in small scale industries—Charka, Ghani and all that. I, on the other hand, led a fairly comfortable life and believed in the industrialization of the country through large scale industry.[12]

Patel, writes Birla, had a similar relationship with Gandhi:

> [Patel] too had his independent views and yet, in every move, political or social, followed the lead of his Master. He quarreled with him privately and followed him publicly. It is curious that many high men in India differed from Gandhi, yet followed him often blindly.[13]

Nehru's chafing at the Mahatma's psychic coercion has already been cited. Only Bajaj did not chafe, although he too had his discontents.

The ambivalence that these leaders experienced in their

relations to Gandhi was settled in his favor by a variety of factors, some common to all of them, some specific to the needs of different men. A common theme that kept restless co-leaders in camp were the para-kinship relations that obtained between Gandhi and them, relations that endured with the inevitability of ascriptive ties beyond any particular issue or encounter. A second, related to the first, is Gandhi's persistent, and sometimes insistent, cultivation of the intimacy that bound him to the co-leaders. A third is his capacity for relevance, for attaching some part of his current program to that in his follower which would be responsive to it.

The para-kinship relations were, in all four cases except Patel's, structured on a filial model, a fact which I would attribute less to a mutual desire for asymmetry than to the fact that three of the four were much younger—Birla by twenty-five years and Nehru and Bajaj by twenty. Patel, who was only two years younger, and Motilal Nehru (to whom I refer because he provides useful contrast), who was eight years older, did not adopt the father-son mode.

Bajaj and Birla explicitly styled the relationship in parafamilial fashion, as father and son. This is most explicit in the case of Bajaj. Adopted as a small boy by an aging merchant-caste father whose son had died without issue, he had felt the want of both a father and a spiritual guide. Sometime after meeting Gandhi, he asked to be made his fifth son, a wish which Gandhi granted and took seriously. Birla too recognized father-son features in his relationship with Gandhi. And even Nehru, assimilated to Western cultural styles in which explicit filial formulations are a less frequent model for non-kin relations, thought of Gandhi as Bapu. The British journalistic fancy which characterized Motilal, Jawaharlal and Gandhi as Father, Son and Holy Ghost was not psychologically blasphemous.

The familism went much further. With his role as political teacher or leader, Gandhi assumed aspects of the status of joint family elder in all the cases before us, rendering advice, suggesting alternatives, and making arrangements. Thus, the thirty-four year old Jawaharlal, who had given up the too practical law for full-time politics, chafed at being dependent on his father financially. In response to the problem, Gandhi explored the possibility of pay for political work and soothed the son. Birla's brother, in consequence of an unconventional marriage, became embroiled in a hassle that split the Birla caste community. Gandhi advised decent fighting tactics and firmness. Another example is how Patel's children's health, education and life arrangements became more the concern of Gandhi than Patel.[14] Not to be overlooked are detailed doctoring and advice on diet and health that pervade Gandhi's letters which allow one to pursue the adventures of nationalist intestines over thirty years. Such para-kinship relations among political figures are not peculiar to Gandhi. They are a frequent, even normal, feature in Indian leader-follower relations. What Gandhi brought to them was a more intense version of the norm.

Kinship, and para-kinship insofar as it succeeds, are ascriptive. But intimacy has to be cultivated. This cultivation was one of Gandhi's specialties and must account for the duration of relations that might otherwise have collapsed—as those with Patel, which were often under strain from Patel's inattentiveness. One has the sense that Patel, having placed himself with the Mahatma, often wished that the Mahatma would leave him alone, especially in matters where they differed greatly—as in Hindu-Muslim relations and in Patel's totally cold-eyed *Realpolitik* orientation. He wished to be left alone, because Gandhi, like political and other saints, had the psychological advantage of righteousness which could best be combated by evasion. But leave him alone was the one thing Gandhi would not do. His intimacy was as assiduous as everything else about him.

Finally, Gandhi had a knack for relevancy, for matching a follower's interest to the possibilities of his social and political program. One instance will serve as illustration. Birla and the Mahatma had begun their more intimate relationship over the tussle in Birla's caste. Gandhi was in search of financial support for his untouchability work, and since he intended to reform from above by persuasion, he needed an eminent public figure close enough to orthodoxy to communicate with it. Birla seemed a likely candidate by virtue of his wealth and by virtue of the merchant-caste traditions of charity. Gandhi attached the meaning of untouchability work to the meaning of Birla's own caste confrontation. Birla wrote: "My own experience as an outcast from any community greatly increased my sympathies with the 'depressed classes,' and made me most willing to further Bapu's campaign for the *Harijans*."[15]

These are some common themes in Gandhi's relations with the co-leaders. Together, they suggest ways in which the intimacy of the relations Gandhi bore to the ashramites was transferred, minus much of the asymmetry, to more political relations and contexts. They do not convey the variety in the relationships with the co-leaders. Particular themes that account for maintaining the relationships were, of course, specific to individuals. Motilal Nehru was held through his son but also by his high estimate of Gandhi's talent as lawyer and investigator. Patel came to Gandhi out of regard for his party organizational work which allowed him to tender important public service. Nehru, the idealistic second-generation son following a pragmatic, successful first-generation father, responded to Gandhi's unconventional anti-establishmentarianism. An aristocrat found a guide to the people. Birla found in him that combination of religious vocation and hardheaded worldliness which is a theme among west Indian merchant castes from Jhunjhunu to Kathiawad. Bajaj was in search of a guru.

These features, which abbreviate Gandhi's meaning to the four men, run a wide gamut from the relatively impersonal qualification of legal talent to the intensely personal one of guru. They suggest the affective range of Gandhi's mind and psyche, and they help explain how and why he was followed.

NOTES

1. For a discussion of such features, see Lloyd I. Rudolph and Susanne Hoeber Rudolph, *The Modernity of Tradition: Political Development in India* (Chicago: University of Chicago Press, 1967), Part II, "The Traditional Roots of Charisma: Gandhi."

2. Donald W. Ferrell, "The Rowlatt Satyagraha in Delhi, 30 March to 18 April, 1919" (unpublished manuscript, Department of History, Institute of Advance Studies, Australia National University).

3. Anil Bhatt, "Caste and Political Mobilisation in a Gujarat District," in Ranji Kothari, ed. *Caste in Indian Politics* (Bombay: Orient Longmans, 1970). B. B. Mishra, *Select Documents on Mahatma Gandhi's Movement in Champaran 1917-18* (Patna: Government of Bihar, 1963) provides materials on the Champaran Movement as does Girish Mishra, "Socio-Economic Background of Gandhi's Champaran Movement," *The Indian Economic and Social History Review* 5 (September 1968): 245-75.

4. Krishnadas (pseud. of Charuchandra Guha), *Seven Months with Gandhi* (Madras: Triplicane, 1928), pp. 36-37.

5. Brij Krishna Chandiwala, *At the Feet of Bapu* (Ahmedabad: Navajivan Publishing House, 1954), p. 68.

6. Introduction to Balvant Sinha, *Under the Shelter of Bapu* (Ahmedabad: Navajivan Publishing House, 1962), p. vii.

7. Chandiwala, *At the Feet of Bapu,* p. 6.

8. Arthur Koestler, *The Lotus and the Robot* (New York: Macmillan, 1961), p. 157.

9. Jawaharlal Nehru, *An Autobiography* (London: The Bodley Head, 1942), p. 539. The quotation appears in one of two chapters of the autobiography, "Paradoxes" and "Conversion or Compulsion," which constitute Nehru's systematic and

extremely fundamental criticism of Gandhi's ideas, strategy, and style.

10. For a discussion of the relationship between a spiritual director and his pupil, see Erik Erikson, *Young Man Luther: A Study in Psychoanalysis and History* (New York: W. W. Norton, 1958), pp. 161-67.

11. Bal Ram Nanda, *The Nehrus* (London: Allen and Unwin, 1962). See also Jawaharlal Nehru, *A Bunch of Old Letters* (Bombay: Asia Publishing House, 1958).

12. G. D. Birla, *In the Shadow of the Mahatma* (Bombay: Orient Longmans, 1955), p. xv.

13. *Ibid.,* p. xviii.

14. Mohandas K. Gandhi, *Letters to Sardar V. Patel* (Ahmedabad: Navajivan Publishing House, 1957), pp. 252-53.

15. Birla, *In the Shadow of the Mahatma,* p. 10.

3

THE FUNCTION
OF GANDHI IN INDIAN NATIONALISM

"The Mahatma I must leave to his fate."
(Gandhi in *Young India*, March 17, 1927)

Ainslie T. Embree

"That which is permanent and, therefore, neces-
sary, eludes the historian of events. Truth transcends history."
Gandhi's judgment, based on his eclectic reading during his imprisonment in 1922-23, is a warning to the historian. This is particularly true when the question he seeks to answer—"what was
Gandhi's role in the growth and development of Indian nationalism?"—so clearly asserts a concern with an interpretation of
historical events quite explicitly denied by Gandhi's assertion
that "names and forms matter little, they come and go."[1] It is
with names and forms that the historian of politics must deal.
In this context the truth and relevance of Gandhi's teachings are
relegated to the background.

There is no denying that the period of Indian history from
1920 to 1942 is the Age of Gandhi. Yet, whole areas of life that
were of enormous importance for modern India were not greatly
influenced by Gandhi. Take, for example, the three documents
that define the constitutional development of modern India: the
Montagu-Chelmsford reforms of 1919, the 1935 Act, and the Constitution of 1950. Gandhi obviously appeared too late on the scene
to have influenced the provisions of the first, and even its imple-

mentation was perhaps not as much affected by the Congress policies of the 1920's as is usually supposed. As for the 1935 Act, it can be argued that it might have been passed earlier, and with most of the same provisions, if it had not been for Gandhi's activities in the 1930's, particularly in relation to the Round Table Conferences. Even the revision of the Communal Award cannot be used as wholly convincing evidence for his influence on the 1935 Constitution. And as for the Constitution of the Republic of India, how many clauses require reference to Gandhi for their explication? Perhaps the strictures against untouchability would not have been expressed in the particular form they are. Still, it is unlikely that any modern constitution would lack a declaration that the fundamental equality of all citizens could not be abrogated by any overt discriminatory mechanisms.

In the economic sphere, there is scarcely more evidence of Gandhi's impact either in the Gandhian age itself or since 1947. India's Green Revolution of the 1960's is rooted in the modernizing processes that are part of world history, not in the Indian nationalist movement led by Gandhi. Take education, another aspect of Indian development for which Gandhi had a special concern. One need not press the point that the educational structure was not changed in any fundamental way from 1920 to 1947 and that its vast expansion since 1947 has followed with remarkable consistency the patterns established in the nineteenth century.

But this exercise in denial of Gandhian influence in specific areas only highlights the fact of his quite extraordinary dominance of the imagination of India—and the world—from 1920 to 1945. An explanation of his role in Indian nationalism will be attempted by way of the broad generalization that Gandhi's political approach—his policies, his ethics, his methods, his whole life style— made it possible for persons from every strata of Indian society to find that self-identification with the destiny of the country which is at the heart of nationalism. According to Erik Erikson, identity is "a process located in the core of the individual and yet also in the core of his communal culture."[2] One need not elaborate on how painful the process of national identification is in a society where the rulers are alien. It is possible to draw up a balance sheet that proves India benefitted materially by alien rule, but no one can doubt that there, as elsewhere, colonial rule exacted a price in psychological distortion, the depth and meaning of which has never been fully analyzed.

Of special significance for this problem of identification with a national culture was the fact that a modern administrative structure had been created in India by the end of the nineteenth century. Such a structure was a precondition for nationalism, since as one political analyst has put it, "the building of the state comes first, and it is within the political framework that the nation comes into being."[3] But Indian nationalists could not appropriate the political framework to their full advantage—as did nationalists in Japan, for example—because it was the product of alien rule. Here as elsewhere Indian nationalists were faced by a painful dilemma: to embrace the forces of modernity, including the political framework, was to endorse the institutions that, in British eyes, legitimized foreign rule. Yet many of the things which they opposed, such as the seeming injustices and inequities of the social system, were rooted in the structure of Indian society itself. This condition produced what was perhaps a unique situation in any major nationalist movement—the attitudes and institutions that the Indian nationalists demanded were products of alien rule, while those they most unanimously deplored were functions of their own culture. The outward symbol of this dilemma was the loyal address to the throne presented at the beginning of each Congress Session. This was not, as is now sometimes suggested, a gesture born of expediency, but a most explicit statement of intellectual commitment.

Here Louis Hartz's analysis of aspects of American history in terms of the "fragment" thesis is pertinent. His argument is that after fragments of the European liberal tradition were ripped from the integral whole and transposed to America, in the new environment quite different kinds of developments took place from what might have been expected. In fact, often the "fragments" were transformed.[4] The fragments of nineteenth century

European, or more specifically, British, political culture transported to India and appropriated by the early nationalists were of profound significance for Indian political development. It is probably not too great an exaggeration to say that this political culture remained up to at least the 1950's the most pervasive element in Indian intellectual life.

The Terrorist Movement in Bengal and the violent reactions against British rule in Maharashtra which reached their climax around 1905 were attempts to solve the nationalist dilemma by freeing Indian nationalism from the sterility of European elements through the use of religious emotionalism, which in India, as elsewhere, has as one of its indispensable components an exaltation of violence and suffering. Beautifully appropriate symbols were at hand in both areas: in Bengal in the religious myth of the Divine Mother who demanded sacrifice, and in Maharashtra in the historical myth of the Warrior King, Shivaji, who had roused his people against an alien oppressor.

Why the nationalist movement did not move towards a full scale acceptance of violence is one of the least explored aspects of modern Indian history, but surely a major factor was that revolution was not acceptable to the majority of the urban educated classes—the lawyers, the doctors, the teachers, the journalists, the businessmen, and the Government servants. Even taken together, these groups were, as the British never wearied of saying, a minuscule minority. But what the British did not recognize was that this minority comprised the articulate leadership, and was, therefore, in a strictly political sense, the only segment of the population which was of importance. These groups were "collaborators," to use the term in a non-pejorative sense.[5] Not just their livelihoods, but what can perhaps best be described as their psychological commitments, were to the patterns of political and intellectual life associated with British rule. When Gandhi declared in 1921 that he had tendered loyal and voluntary assistance to the Government for an unbroken period of nearly thirty years in the full belief that this was the path to freedom for his country,[6] he was writing the biography of the articulate Western educated classes, not just making an autobiographical statement.

Violent revolution demands complete commitment to a method as well as to a cause. There is no half-way house in a revolutionary movement that has resolved on violence. It is not a method that is possible for those who want to keep to their old moorings, either spiritual or physical. Gandhi provided another possibility—the way of nonviolence. In simplest terms his grand achievement was to persuade very large and influential segments of the Indian population that the truth of India's history was to be found through interpreting it as a search for a nonviolent confrontation between man and man and man and the state. From this outlook grew a nationalist ideology that permitted Indians to link their personal identity with the core of communal culture. Ultimately, the Gandhian path may have demanded as complete a commitment as did the path of revolutionary violence. At the same time there was always the possibility of readjustments and withdrawal.

Commentators on the New Testament have often argued that the essential thrust of its ethical teachings is that they are unrealizable in any conceivable human situation—hence their applicability to all situations. Since no one can fulfill the rigor of their demands completely, any measure of attainment can be accepted. So with the Gandhian ideology. It is eschatological with non-historical ends. The ideology appeared as a solution to the dilemmas and perplexities of the Indian situation—not so much because it was ambiguous—but because despite rigorous demands it made possible all levels of involvement. The constitutional gradualism of the pioneers foreclosed participation in a whole range of political activity from throwing bombs to refusing to exercise the franchise provided in the 1919 constitution. Similarly, in a violent revolution in which evasion and concealment are necessary, lines are ultimately drawn from which there is no easy retreat. Perhaps the unique, and ironic, characteristic of the Indian nationalist movement is that the transition to participation in the post-independence period was easiest for those who up to 1947 had remained either neutral or actual supporters of the old regime.

R. C. Majumdar has argued with learning and passion that an honest historian must admit that Gandhi was lacking in both political wisdom and political sagacity, "and far from being infallible, committed serious blunders, one after another, in pursuit of some Utopian ideals and methods which had no basis in reality."[7] Majumdar is probably correct, but it was precisely the Utopian ideals that prevented the growth in India of the deep and lasting antagonisms that have characterized almost all other nationalist movements. There is, of course, a seemingly glaring contradiction to this statement in the growth of Muslim separatism. But while this movement was an aspect of nationalism, it had roots in prenationalist history. As will be suggested later, Muslim separatism was an alternative nationalism, not a split within the main tradition.

Related to the generalization that one major explanation of the appeal of the Gandhian ideology is that it permitted allegiance and identification with varying degrees of commitment is another: that Gandhi effectively prevented class divisions from finding political roles in Indian nationalism. For Indian socialists of the 1920's and 1930's, this was the clearest proof of the reactionary direction of his leadership, and the bitterness of their denunciation of Gandhi masked their despair as they recognized the failure of their own appeal.[8]

Gandhi's peculiar genius lay, then, in his understanding of how the complex fabric of traditional Indian society could be related to the essentially modern phenomenon of the movement for political independence. He was not the "father of his country" in the sense that he initiated the nationalist movement, for the groundwork had been laid long before he appeared on the scene. What he did was to give the masses for the first time a sense of involvement in the nation's destiny while persuading the old leaders to accept his leadership. The Rowlatt Acts, Jallianwala

Bagh, and the Khilafat issue provided the setting for this change in direction./

The violent opposition to the Rowlatt Acts in all sections of the Indian political world was a reflection of the curious relationship that still existed between the Indian nationalists and the Government. There was remarkably little recognition that if, as the nationalists asserted, the British were merely an occupying power, then the Rowlatt Acts were precisely the kind of legislation they might be expected to pass. Gandhi's own commitment to action within a legal framework was shaken. The Government itself had moved outside this framework by passing laws that were "unjust, subversive of the principles of liberty and justice and destructive of the elementary rights of individuals on which the safety of the community as a whole and the state itself is based."[9] His remedy was to call for the one-day *hartal*, which, along with the defiance of the prohibitions against public meetings, led to Jallianwala Bagh.

Political leaders of all persuasions denounced the Amritsar massacre. But not all of them agreed that the time had come to end attempts at cooperation. Rabindranath Tagore feared that India would be caught up in the same demonic force of nationalism that was destroying the West. He warned Gandhi that the violence that had followed the first *hartal* had shown that "power in all its forms is irrational. . . . Passive resistance is a force that is not necessarily moral in itself: it can be used against truth as well as for it."[10]

Gandhi had come to somewhat the same conclusion as he heard of outbreaks of violence that were occurring throughout the country. He called for an end of the strike, and when the Congress held its annual session at Amritsar in December 1919, he led the fight for a decision to cooperate with the Government by helping to work for the new constitution. This was a direct challenge to the old Extremists and their supporters who were for refusing any further compromises. Attending his last session of the Congress, Tilak argued for denunciation of the constitution. But Gandhi carried the day, and the resolution approving cooperation was passed.

Within a year Gandhi was to make what seemed a complete about face: he led the Congress into the non-cooperation movement, rejecting all the forms of participation in the constitutional framework he had persuaded the nationalists to accept in December 1919. The report of the Hunter Commission and the growing unrest among Muslims associated with the Khilafat movement were the immediate determinants of this new direction in Gandhi's leadership. His sense of timing convinced him that the moment for a confrontation with the government had come. He saw in the anti-British sentiment engendered by the Khilafat dispute the possibility of a rapprochment with the Islamic community as well as a means to win acceptance of satyagraha.

To those who reminded him of the violence, including the dreadful events at Amritsar, which followed the first experiments in satyagraha in April 1919, Gandhi replied that no country has ever risen without being purified through the fire of suffering and India could not escape from slavery without paying the costs of self-purification.[11] This reference to suffering is important in the history of Indian nationalism. Blood and iron were the traditional weapons for forging national identity, and Gandhi recognized that sacrifice, beyond the sacrifice of hard work or even prison terms, would be necessary. Blood must be shed, but in a transvaluation of nationalist values, it would be the blood of the righteous. *Swaraj,* self-rule, would be the fruit of sacrifice.

Gandhi gave no definition of *swaraj,* and the vagueness was perhaps deliberate. For the educated classes, deeply committed to Western political institutions, it meant democratic, parliamentary government on the British model; for Gandhi it had an almost apolitical meaning. "Abandonment of the fear of death," or "the ability to regard every inhabitant of India as our own brother or sister," were some of the definitions he used in an attempt to give content to the term.[12] Fundamentally, his own life style reflected the term's values.

During this time the Congress had to make basic decisions

about Indian nationhood. The emphasis was no longer on hurting the British or even on making India strong through home industries; the demand was for a radical reorientation of national life. Speaking for the intellectual elite, Rabindranath Tagore sensed that the anti-intellectual and anti-rational elements might combine with the emphasis on the Indian past to frustrate the growth of community based on reason and mutual understanding. "Our present struggle to alienate our heart and mind from the West," he wrote, "is an attempt at spiritual suicide."[13]

The Gandhian message was thus for many in 1920 a call to renounce that search for accommodation with the modern world which had been the hallmark of the nationalist movement and to replace it with an inward-looking vision of traditional Indian society, purified and cleansed, but nevertheless pre-modern and pre-industrial. The implementation of the policy of non-cooperation accepted by the Congress in 1920 meant the abandonment of its historic stance as the "loyal opposition," seeking to persuade and educate the Government, not to coerce it. And while they were being asked to give up opportunities for exercising power through participation in the new legislative councils, they were being told at the same time that they must renounce the use of violence, the alternative method used with telling effect against the British in the early years of the century by the Bengal revolutionaries.

Complicating the call to renounce the modern world was the seeming contradiction of the very considerable support Gandhi received from the great industrialists of western India, notably the textile manufacturers. A cynical explanation is that they saw in Gandhi a power that could free them from the competition of European industries. Another explanation may be as important. Many of the industrialists of western India were drawn from the traditional trading classes and were far less alienated from tradition than the educated elite of Calcutta and its environs. Gandhi appealed to this sense of tradition. He helped them to fulfill their classic role as men of affairs who recognize saintliness and are willing to pay for its upkeep but do not feel compelled to emulate it. But they were modern men, too, in many ways, more so than the intellectuals—the lawyers, journalists, teachers—who had shaped the early phases of nationalism. The anti-intellectualism of the Gandhian movement which Tagore deplored was more than obscurantism rooted in the past. It was also an expression of the values of the business and commercial classes which were becoming a potent force in Indian political life. The old nationalist movement had drawn both its leadership and its support from a relatively small segment of society, and the success of the Gandhian movement in reaching out to new groups inevitably made for tension.

The 1921 movement had awakened a response throughout India. The masses had often been stirred before, for nothing is more false to the realities of Indian society than to picture it as apathetic and unmoved. Its susceptibility to passionate involvement is attested by a multitude of religious movements and sectarian groups. But in 1921 this capacity for passion—and, Gandhi argued, for suffering—was harnessed to the aims of a nationalist organization.

A sense of excitement, of new possibilities for India, led many individuals to perform dramatic acts of self-sacrifice in the service of the nationalist cause. More important was the involvement of the non-heroic and the partially committed. The spinning of thread and the wearing of khadi were an integral part of this program. The simple white "Gandhi cap" became a symbol of support for the national cause. In a country of extraordinary diversity of dress and manners, the adoption of such an easily recognizable symbol was a stroke of genius. The spinning of thread might not do much to alter economic conditions, but the experience of working together in great mass meetings gave people an exhilarating sense of participation in the political process. So did another of the common features of the movement—the burning of foreign cloth. Gandhi's defense of this practice, which seemed to many so wasteful in a land where people went naked because they could not afford clothing, exhibited the blend of passionate religious imagery and practical common sense that was at once appealing and confusing. It was sinful to wear foreign clothing, he said, "when I know that if I had but worn the things woven by the neighboring spinners and weavers, that would have clothed me, and fed and clothed them. On the knowledge of my sins bursting upon me, I must consign the foreign garments to the flames and thus purify myself. . . . In burning my foreign clothes, I burn my shame."[14]

One of Gandhi's most important innovations was the involvement of women in the nationalist movement. Telling them that the economic and moral salvation of India rested with them, Gandhi appealed to them to set an example of self-denial, to give up the use of foreign goods both for themselves and their children. The patriotic woman will "refuse to adorn herself for men, including her husband, if she will be an equal partner with men."[15] This was a new, and exciting, message. Traditional Indian society emphasized the necessity of the good woman submitting herself to her husband's wishes, although it exalted her role as mother and giver of life. Gandhi's declaration that women could achieve an equality with men, or even in fact, a kind of superiority, through methods based upon the most time-honored concepts of wifely duty, had a profound psychological appeal. Furthermore, the virtues that Gandhi extolled as the basis of *swaraj* were those he associated with classic Indian life. Meekness and obedience were the other side of strength and courage. The female sex is "the nobler of the two, for it is the embodiment of sacrifice, silent suffering, humility, faith and knowledge."[16]

Gandhi appealed to the masses of Indian women, but the ones who responded most strongly, and took part in political life in ways perhaps unmatched by women anywhere else in the world, were women of the upper and middle classes. Here was a reservoir of intelligence and skill which had never before been tapped for the national cause, and thousands of women found release from the stultifying boredom of the routines of upper-class Indian life by throwing themselves into the Gandhian movement. They became his ardent disciples, providing him with unpaid assistants for organizational work and stirring society by their willingness to march in processions and go to jail. Their reward was high office and influence.

By 1922, Gandhi was playing for high stakes: continuance of at least a facade of unity between the various factions in the Congress as well as with the Muslims. He realized that to stop the non-cooperation program and begin negotiations with the British would lose the Muslims. There were also groups in the Congress as well as among the Muslims who were advocating open defiance of British power. Gandhi's answer to those who wanted peace through accommodation was, "I am a man of peace, but I do not want peace that you find in a grave." His answer to the militants was the reminder that their program "did not admit the weakest of your brothers."[17] Behind the epigrammatic ellipsis was his conviction that the non-cooperation program was validated by its ability to include all sorts and conditions of men.

Then came the killings at Chauri Chaura and Gandhi's decision to do what he had refused to do a few months before— to call off the movement. This action, which seemed so inexplicable at the time, was the product of something more than a quixotic intuition. Gandhi's religious idiom suggested that his main concern was the inviolate purity of the doctrine of non-violence as a political technique, but this masked a shrewd assessment of the realities of Indian life. The violence at Chauri Chaura had convinced him that he must go slow, for he knew that the poverty and frustration of Indian life made violence endemic. He was an anarchist in his view of the perfect society, but he had no expectation that the destruction of the existing order could lead to anything but new forms of tyranny. He had meant what he said, he insisted, when he had promised *swaraj* in a year— but only if there were a change of heart on the part of the people. From the standpoint of his ethical theories, the pervasive violence of the past year had shown that the people were not yet ready for the purifying experience of satyagraha, of civil disobedience conducted without violence even under the severest provocation.

By 1922, Gandhi knew that the majority of the leaders were no longer with him and that the enormous popularity he enjoyed among the masses was very often based upon a false image of his power and his intentions. "I know that the only thing that the Government dreads," he wrote, "is this huge majority I seem to command. They little know that I dread it even more than they." He was a prisoner of the violence and frustration that had found a focus in the national movement, and by this time he was "actually and literally praying for a disastrous defeat."[18] The obvious defeat would be his arrest. In his own religious terminology, this would be a purification; in political terms, it would give him time to redefine his purposes and regroup his forces for another noncooperation movement.

Only someone who was wholly immersed in the tradition, but who had also looked at it from outside, could have used it so intuitively. The prison sentence became part of the drama of renunciation and suffering he had envisaged as the way India must follow to find true freedom. Prison became the substitute for the banishment to the forest that plays the central role in the great legends of India, where the hero accepts the sentence gracefully and turns the forest into a spiritual retreat from which he returns tested, strengthened, and purified. Gandhi returned from his prison exile, confident that the future was with him, not with those who were seeking to redirect the nationalist movement back into the old channels through participation in the legislative assemblies and the other institutions set up by the administration. For the next twenty years the tensions between the two interpretations—the Gandhian insistence on social salvation through personal commitment over against the policies of institutional participation—governed the development of Indian nationality.

But by the end of the 1920's, a tension of a different order emerged from the growth of Muslim separatism. There is no space here to study the effect of Gandhi's dominance in the Congress on Muslim politics, but a brief comment may serve to relate the Age of Gandhi to the Age of Jinnah. A common explanation, which sees a direct causal connection, is that since Gandhi gave a Hindu vocabulary, a Hindu coloration, to Indian nationalism, the Muslims were inevitably alienated. That Gandhi continually expressed his belief in the truth of all religions is undeniable, but this declaration was in itself the most Hindu of statements. One is tempted to say that it is almost the only dogma of modern Hinduism. Its assertion had the wholly unintended effect, it is argued, of alienating Muslims whose fundamental dogma was an explicit denial of Gandhi's inclusiveness. A related argument is that the estrangement of the Muslims sprang partly at least from Gandhi's inability, which he shared with most Hindus, of understanding that Muslims, like Christians, find their identity (or in religious terms, their salvation) through membership in a community that is by definition the guardian and arbiter of "truth." Their ultimate loyalties must be to this community, neither the *swaraj* of Gandhi nor the secular democracy of Nehru.

Both these explanations of Gandhi's influence on Muslim participation in the major institution of nationalist identity, the Indian National Congress, have much to commend them, but they argue from the basic presupposition of that body. That is, they assume that Muslim separatism was an evil and that its growth could have, and should have, been prevented. Such a premise is, of course, utterly unacceptable to Muslim separatists; it betrays, they argue, the very Hindu insensitivity that made a united India impossible. But Muslim separatists, including Jinnah himself, did not denounce Gandhi for his use of a religious vocabulary. On the contrary, they applauded him for his honesty in demonstrating that the Congress was a Hindu organization. The other reality, Jinnah insisted, was the existence of a Muslim nation in India.

Jinnah's logic seems unimpeachable—Gandhi, no more than the British, could have created Muslim separatism. Its components existed within the fabric of Indian culture and historical experience in exactly the same way as did the mainstream of nationalism represented by the Congress. The movement represented by the Muslim League, and for which Jinnah was the elegant spokesman, was an alternative Indian nationalism, a legitimate variant to that articulated by the Congress and Gandhi. It offered to

Muslims the possibility of a fusion of personal identity with a cultural core in the same way the Congress did to the majority of Indians. Muslim separatism served another function for which it is seldom given credit: its existence as an opposition undoubtedly helped Gandhi maintain control over the disparate and warring fiefs within the Congress.

Gandhi's relations with the Muslims were matched in some ways by his involvement with untouchability, with Dr. Ambedkar seeking to become the Jinnah, as it were, of the millions who had been excluded from participation in the dominant civic and religious culture. That the climax to Gandhi's challenge to the ancient system came in a simultaneous confrontation with the British government and Ambedkar was the result of skillful political strategy as well as of his passionate concern for Indian unity.

The occasion was the award of seventy-one seats in the provincial councils, a decision made in response to Dr. Ambedkar's demands for protection of the "untouchables" as a minority over against the caste Hindus. Gandhi's announcement that he would fast to the death unless the award was withdrawn created a dilemma for the British who feared that Gandhi's death might trigger an outburst of violence the Government of India could not contain. It also placed Ambedkar in a difficult position, for he and his followers would be held responsible.

For Gandhi the award of seats to the untouchables would be a further division of Indian society, perpetuating the inferiority of the *Harijans* by giving them a vested interest in not changing their status. Ambedkar denounced this as a thinly veiled argument for using the seventy million untouchables as weightage for the Hindus against the Muslims. As the attention of the nation focused once more on Gandhi, an intricate agreement was worked out. In essence, it assured *Harijan* representatives twice as many places in the legislative councils but did not give them separate constituencies. These results led to division within Congress ranks, with pragmatic leaders like Subhas Chandra Bose seeing no gains for anyone in the new formula, and the strong

Hindu wing of the Congress regarding it as one more betrayal of Indian culture.

By directing his own attention and that of many of his followers into the campaign against untouchability, Gandhi no doubt drew off some of the energy that might have gone into more directly political purposes. But his concern for what he regarded as an intolerable blot on Hindu society stirred the imagination and the conscience of the Indian people. His ceaseless travels from village to village throughout the country was a modern version of the paradigm of the traditional, wandering Hindu saint in quest of salvation both for himself and for those who thronged to see him. Even his insistence that everyone, including the poorest people, should give him some contribution for the national cause was rooted in the elemental feeling that both the giving and receiving of alms are marks of spiritual grace.

After 1934, the history of the nationalist movement is singularly confused, with many of the decisions appearing to be hopelessly wrongheaded. After all the protests and denunciations of the 1935 Act, there was a return to the Assembly and the provincial councils as there had been in 1922. A confrontation with the Government had been sought and then avoided. At the same time, there was a refusal to enter into serious discussion with the Government on the Constitution the Congress finally agreed to operate. Cooperation with the Muslim League through the formation of coalition ministries was rejected almost out of hand. There was always a failure to take the Muslim League seriously, an easy assumption that it was not, as it claimed, an alternative nationalism. A more generous understanding, critics argue, might have saved India from 1947 and its aftermath.

Gandhi was deeply involved in the main decisions. But what the critics ignore is that perhaps the complexity of India's political and cultural inheritance would not have permitted any easier transition to independence. Gandhi's influence may have led to some major errors in political strategy, but one is left with the impression that he made the right mistakes, completing one stage of the long process of defining a nation. "Who and what are the real Indian people?" Lord Curzon asked in 1905.[19] His answer was that insofar as one could speak of an Indian people, one meant the peasant masses, who found their identity not as Indians but as Punjabis or Bengalis or Madrasis, and that the slogans of the nationalists were utterly meaningless to them. That to some extent Curzon's question could be answered differently in 1947 was not due to Gandhi alone. But one dares to venture the opinion that no other leader in history in his own lifetime had done so much to make a people into a nation.

NOTES

1. Quoted in D. G. Tendulkar, *Mahatma* (New Delhi: Publications Division, Government of India, 1961), 2:3.
2. Erik Erikson, *Identity: Youth and Crisis* (New York: W. W. Norton, 1968), p. 22.
3. Carl Friedrich, *Man and His Government* (New York: McGraw-Hill, 1963), p. 547.
4. Louis Hartz, *The Liberal Tradition in America,* and *The Founding of New Societies* (New York: Harcourt Brace, 1955 and 1964).
5. See Anil Seal, *The Emergence of Indian Nationalism* (London: Cambridge University Press, 1968), for an interesting analysis of nationalism in terms of "collaboration."
6. *Young India,* February 9, 1921.
7. R. C. Majumdar, *History of the Freedom Movement in India* (Calcutta: Firma K. L. Mukhopadhyay, 1963), 3: xviii-xix.
8. M. N. Roy, *Fragments of a Prisoner's Diary* (Calcutta: Renaissance Publications, 1950), 2:190-236.

9. Satyagraha Pledge, February 24, 1919, in Tendulkar, *Mahatma,* 1:241.
10. Quoted in *Ibid.,* 2:51.
11. *Young India,* June 16, 1920.
12. Quoted in B. R. Nanda, *Mahatma Gandhi* (London: Allen and Unwin, 1958), p. 205.
13. Tagore to C. F. Andrews, quoted in J. H. Broomfield, *Elite Conflict in a Plural Society* (Berkeley: University of California Press, 1968), p. 150.
14. *Young India,* October 13, 1921.
15. Quoted in Tendulkar, *Mahatma,* 2:50.
16. Quoted in *Ibid.,* 2:51.
17. Quoted in *Ibid.,* 2:72.
18. *Young India,* March 2, 1922.
19. Quoted in Sir Thomas Raleigh, *Lord Curzon in India* (London: Macmillan, 1906), pp. 584-85.

THE IDEAS OF GANDHI AND THEIR
TRANSMISSION

4

THE THEORY
AND PRACTICE OF *SARVODAYA*

Nirmal Kumar Bose

It was in South Africa that Gandhi first read Ruskin's *Unto This Last*. The book led to an immediate transformation in his way of life. Later he prepared a paraphrase of the book in Gujarati and published it in *Indian Opinion* which he had founded in South Africa to help the cause of satyagraha. The Gujarati version bore the title of "*Sarvodaya*." Literally, the word means "the welfare of all" in contrast to the concept of "the greatest good of the greatest number." To bring out the distinction clearly, Gandhi wrote in 1926:

> A votary of *ahimsa* cannot subscribe to the utilitarian formula. He will strive for the greatest good of all and die in the attempt to realize the ideal. He will, therefore, be willing to die so that the others may live. He will serve himself with the rest by himself dying. The greatest good of all inevitably includes the good of the greatest number, and therefore he and the utilitarian will converge in many points in their career, but there does come a time when they must part company, and even work in opposite directions. The utilitarian to be logical will never sacrifice himself. The absolutist will even sacrifice himself.[1]

One of the lessons which Gandhi drew from his reading of Ruskin is that the value of all socially useful work is or ought to be the same. He held that the lawyer and the barber should have the same right of earning their livelihood from their work. This would imply an equality of wages, although Gandhi did not make that point specifically. Gandhi also held that a life of manual labor is the best life. Later he developed the idea still further when he began to say that every man should earn his bread by the sweat of his brow, an idea he may have borrowed from Tolstoy.

What would be the place of an intellectual worker in the Gandhian scheme? Gandhi's answer was:

> Intellectual work is important and has an undoubted place in the scheme of life. But what I insist on is the necessity of physical labour. No man, I claim, ought to be free from that obligation. It will serve to improve even the quality of his intellectual output.[2]

The question remains, how was the Gandhian ideal of economic transformation actually going to be achieved? In this regard, Gandhi held very clearly that those who subscribed to the idea of an exploitation-free economic order should begin with a reordering of their own lives. But this was clearly not enough. Institutions had also to be changed. Just as new institutions had to be built up, so any institution which came in the way of the practice of the New Life should also be resisted by means of nonviolent non-cooperation. He was especially concerned to reform capital and labor so that the divisions of society into antagonistic classes would end and be replaced by a common-wealth of harmony.

One special question arises out of Gandhi's view: if a small or a large band of people try to build a nonviolent, exploitation-free economic order, will there be no internal or external opposition to it? How will the community practicing a New Life deal with possible challenges? As a practical idealist, Gandhi recognized the difficulties and developed his own answer to the question of defense. He was often asked: what can be defended by nonviolence? His usual answer was that a community which tried to equip itself for such defense should, first of all, get rid of all illegitimate possessions. It must surrender all the gains of violence and, beyond that, share its resources, both natural and human, with the rest of mankind.

Once while describing his ideal for a nation, he said:

> I want the freedom of my country so that other countries may learn something from my free country, so that the resources of my country might be utilized for the benefit of mankind. . . . My love therefore of nationalism, or my idea of nationalism, is that my country may become free, that if need be, the whole country may die so that the human races may live.[3]

Gandhi firmly held that if a small community began to rebuild its life of work and sharing, and if the facts became duly known to their neighbors, the community would gain a degree of moral stature which would help to spread the good news all over the world. If, even then, there was aggression from within or without, the community would try to defend itself by means of nonviolent non-cooperation. They would refuse to treat the so-called aggressor as anything other than an errring brother and refuse to strike back in self-defense.

The willingness of the nonviolent non-cooperator to share whatever he has with anyone who is genuinely in want, and his quiet courage in the defense of the new order of life, will eventually touch the heart of the aggressor and pave the way for his conversion. Once Gandhi was asked if he really believed that the heart of a tyrant could ever be touched by means of satyagraha. His reply indicated his knowledge, gained through bitter experience, that he himself might fail. But a tyrant acts only through the cooperation of a million soldiers who are no better and no worse than any of us. If their hearts are touched, the tyrant will become isolated, and that would be the utmost that we can hope for. Then, if all the satyagrahis die in the defense of their cause without any visible effect upon the aggressor, that very act of sacrifice will awaken the conscience of the world, and the satyagrahis will have done all that it is possible for them to do.

Even if we accept that the Gandhian method ensures the good of all, *sarvodaya,* the question remains: how do we begin our task? Shall we try to bring about perfection in individuals and small communities and hope that the existing institutions which foster inequality will eventually wither away and fall down like dead leaves in autumn? Tolstoy, whom Gandhi regarded as one of the great teachers of mankind, was undoubtedly of such an opinion. He said that every individual should go on perfecting his own life by living in accordance with the true precepts of Christianity. One should not resist evil. One should totally disregard the state which is altogether an evil. But Gandhi differed from him in one very important respect. Although he wanted individuals, in combination, to try to build up the New Life, yet Gandhi also held that we must resist evil institutions to preserve our own. The resistance should be by moral and faultless means.

Even in the midst of the stiffest of nonviolent campaigns in India, Gandhi took great pains to remind those who were in the thick of the fight that our war was not against communities but against institutions to which they wrongly subscribed. Our object was to wean them from error and, in the same process, to be weaned from our own errors, if there were any. Gandhi held that it was in this way that we should refuse to surrender our sense of brotherhood even in the midst of a struggle, for it was only in this way that we could ensure and promote the good of all.

All through his life in India, Gandhi practiced and propagated the ideal and the method described above. Although for him nonviolence was a creed and a passion, yet when he led the nation in its battles against political or social wrongs, he always recommended formulas of action for the masses which were in conformity with their temper and strength.

In 1921, Gandhi began his constructive program with the promotion of manual textile industries and the establishment of inter-communal amity. His political movement in those days did not rise to a high pitch of militancy. He appeared to be drilling the masses for more difficult battles to come. During the decade of the 1930's he raised the pitch of his constructive activities, adding to the original base such items as craft-centered primary education and efforts for economic equality. The political action of 1930-32 and of 1942 was more challenging. Men and women were then called upon to face the assassin's dagger or bullet without flinching while they were at their appointed task. Thus, India slowly progressed in her exercise of collective nonviolence, until, through historical circumstances, the transfer of power took place from British to Indian hands in mid-1947.

Obviously, Gandhi welcomed British withdrawal. But he was not happy, for partition came with freedom and the *swaraj,* or self-rule of the masses, still remained a distant goal. The constructive program which should have laid the foundation of economic and social emancipation had not been given due attention. It was this, therefore, to which he asked the political workers to turn their minds. In January 1948, Gandhi took one of the most decisive and revolutionary steps in his entire political career. He recommended that the Congress dissolve itself. He asked its members to spread over the seven hundred and fifty thousand villages of India and Pakistan to educate and organize the villagers in their new rights and duties. In effect, the Congress was to be transformed into a Lok Sevak Sangh or Organization for the Service of the People. To complement the change in the party system, economic production and political power were to be decentralized and regulated through panchayats which would embrace one another in ever-widening circles of cooperation.

But the fates seem to have ordained otherwise. Gandhi had overcome the feeling of disillusionment which had cast its shadow over him during the months immediately after independence.

But just when he had decided to take a bold step, he was stricken by the hand of an assassin who believed that he had weakened India by his lessons of nonviolence.

The blow stunned the nation. But thanks to the efforts of Prime Minister Jawaharlal Nehru, the Government took a very firm stand to curb further communal disturbances and to govern effectively. After Gandhi's death many people realized that national integration should be fostered with greater care. As part of that objective, the division between Hindu and Moslem as well as between the rich and the poor had to be healed as quickly as possible. The Five-Year Plans of development came one after another to raise the productive capacity of the nation and to elevate the standard of living. These goals had to be achieved through the democratic process, not by totalitarian methods.

One of the unexpected results of governmental action was that the whole country began to lean more and more heavily upon legislative and administrative measures for the achievement of the goal of democratic socialism. The self-reliance which had been an outstanding feature of the nation's activities during three decades of Gandhian leadership appeared to be in retreat. There was hardly any fresh endeavor to build up democracy from the base. Even when local self-government was promoted through Panchayat Raj, and a large part of the community development program was entrusted to it, critical observers discovered that at the local district or village level the class of landed proprietors and moneyed men retained or came into power through the elections. Clearly, this result was the opposite of what Gandhi had wanted through his constructive program and his suggested rule of the panchayats. As a result, many of the political and social workers, who had committed themselves to the Gandhian ideal, suffered from a deep feeling of frustration. They did not have the awareness or the skill to reverse the process which had led the country to an increasing reliance upon the state and the political party for attainment of economic and social goals.

While the developments outlined above were taking place, Vinoba emerged as a new force in another corner of India, far

from Delhi. A fellow worker with Gandhi since 1916, he had dedicated himself without reservation to the cause of nonviolence. Soon after Gandhi's death, in March 1948, there was a meeting of constructive workers in Gandhi's establishment at Wardha. There, on the suggestion of Vinoba, the *Sarvodaya* Samaj, the Society for the Promotion of *Sarvodaya,* came into existence. A year afterwards, the first annual conference was held in Indore where the Sarva Seva Sangh, Association for Service in the Cause of *Sarvodaya,* was formed. The third conference was held in a village near Hyderabad city in 1951. In the meanwhile, Vinoba had sponsored the idea that the constructive workers, as well as people in general, should be freed from their reliance upon money. The vow of freedom from money, *Kanchanmukti,* was taken. When Vinoba went to the conference in Hyderabad, he walked all the way from near Wardha to the place of conference, a distance of 315 miles. Out of this experience came *Bhoodan,* the Land-Gift Movement.

The State of Hyderabad had land problems peculiarly its own. Earlier there were popular risings against the ruling class and a large measure of counterviolence. Eventually, the Government of India intervened, and the Nizam was deposed. Under these disturbed conditions, the Communist Party entered the arena. Their strategy was to seize land from landlords. In the process a reign of terror came to the countryside.

During his journey through the disturbed area, Vinoba came to realize the nature of the problems. To educate himself he had an exchange of views with the Communists. It was then that he decided that the redistribution of land should be brought about in a peaceful way. During a walking tour through the Telengana area, Vinoba reached a village named Pochampalli, inhabited mostly by landless laborers members of the so-called untouchable castes. When asked by Vinoba as to how their problem could be solved, these laborers, consulted one another and said that, if they could secure 80 acres of land for cultivation, they would be satisfied. At the village meeting Vinoba asked if anyone could make this amount of land available. A farmer named V. R. Reddy came forward and donated 100 acres for the use of landless laborers. This was on April 18, 1951.

This event opened up a new concept in Vinoba's mind— *Bhoodan,* the Land-Gift Movement. He believed that other donors like the one at Pochampalli would not be wanting in the country. Indeed, in the fifty-one days of his tour through nearly two hundred villages in the Telengana area, Vinoba secured a gift of 12,201 acres from farmers, both big and small. Month after month, Vinoba proceeded on his walking tour through Hydera-bad, Uttar Pradesh, Bihar, Orissa, Kerala and other states. His program began to unfold. With a shrewd, practical sense Vinoba did not ask for more than one-sixth of the land which any one possessed. His appeal to those who had no land was that they should contribute a number of days in labor or a certain fraction of their earnings every month to be used, on their own initiative, for communal service. The last came to be known as *Sampattidan,* Gift of Property.

News of Vinoba's mission spread widely throughout the country, and many social and political workers responded to the attraction of the movement. In Orissa, Land-Gift was elevated to *Gramdan,* Village-Gift. In *Bhoodan,* the owner retained title to the land which he had not given away. But under *Gramdan,* when nearly three-fourths of the villagers were ready, they surrendered their personal right of property and transferred it to the community organization of the village, *Gramsabha,* Village Association. The Association, formed by the villagers them-selves, was to redistribute the land to the needy. A part of the donated land was to be set aside for communal purposes. Every-one had to contribute his labor for its cultivation, and the pro-duce, or the money obtained from sale, was to meet some of the common needs of the village.

From Land-Gift to Village-Gift, the process has now de-veloped into sub-movements of *Prakhandadan,* Block-Gift, and *Zilladan,* District-Gift. As of April 30, 1969, there were just over 100,000 villages in the *Gramdan* category, 700 Blocks and seven-teen Districts.

An account of the Land-Gift movement would not be complete without mention of J. C. Kumarappa and J. P. Narayan. Trained in economics, Kumarappa led the village industries' organization for several years. A firm believer in decentralization as a means of attaining economic justice and peace, Kumarappa has become, since Gandhi's death, a spokesman for a "Third Order" whose purpose is to ensure equality of land distribution and the adequate development of the land. Some of the Land-Gift workers pin their faith on building up Kumarappa's Third Order. Others believe that dissemination of the concept of Land-Gift is sufficient and that the inhabitants of the donated villages can be left alone to establish their new society.

Jayprakash Narayan is one of our most outstanding leaders. He began his career as a Marxist-Leninist, drifted through Democratic Socialism and since Independence has become one of the most ardent champions of the *sarvodaya* movement. His statement, *From Socialism to Sarvodaya,* is one of the best expressions of the contrast between what Marxist Socialists seek and what Gandhi desired for India. In the course of his passage through Democratic Socialism to *Sarvodaya,* he progressively shed his reliance upon parliaments and parties until he propounded the idea of a party-less democracy. But his major stress is on creating economic democracy from the bottom as proposed by Vinoba. Jayprakash feels confident that the Land-Gift Movement will be able to solve the problem of land through voluntary endeavor much faster than any governmental program can reach a solution. Already, a very large number of workers have been assembled to work in all the states.

In the interim, the central regime and the state governments have passed measure after measure which profoundly influence ownership rights to land. Among the important steps taken have been the abolition of the zemindar system, the recognition of the rights of refugees to lands which they have forcibly occupied, and the enactment of special laws regarding land held or formerly possessed by tribal communities in parts of Bihar and Andhra Pradesh. On the other hand, several branches of the

Communist Party have given priority to the capture by violence or otherwise of land belonging to absentee landlords or owners of tea or coffee plantations. This program is also being extended to landowners who, in the opinion of the Communist Party, hold more land than they require. Cases of liquidation of such land-owning farmers are not rare in the country.

One pressing problem in implementing the Land-Gift Movement is that there is a lack of a sufficient number of workers who can cover all the donated villages to help the people organize their economic life in a new way. Moreover, very few in the movement seem to accept the responsibility of implementing the well-intentioned laws of the state which would be to the advantage of the villagers. Some workers seem to fear contamination by political power. This is not a healthy sign. Another problem is the lack of resistance to land laws which might eventually prove detrimental to the interests of the peasantry. In contrast, Gandhi helped the people to work at both ends. While he promoted reconstruction through non-official agencies, he encouraged the people to take advantage of whatever power had come to them through elections. If resistance to law were indicated, he would not hesitate to urge disobedience in the name of justice.

All the thinking in connection with the Land-Gift Movement seems to have become centered around Vinoba and a handful of his close associates. When Gandhi lived and worked, he was the source of programs and guidance for India. There did not develop any intellectual movement to support, modify or critically examine the Gandhian movement. As a result, when he was no longer there, India drifted towards economic and political models which had little relevance to the actualities of life. Results were produced which were far from what was anticipated. The programs grew out of books, not from the soil.

If today there continues to be an excessive reliance upon one man or even half a dozen men, and if there is no critical assessment of anticipated and actual results, there is ground for fearing that the Land-Gift Movement may gravitate into a routine performance when Vinoba or Jayprakash Narayan are

no longer there to maintain a creative level. In their despair, the masses of India may be driven to other remedies which may eventually lead them to new forms of subordination. Perhaps an enlightened intellect can save us in time from such a predicament.

NOTES

1. Quoted in N. K. Bose, *Selections from Gandhi* (Ahmedabad: Navajivan Publishing House, 1968), p. 37.
2. Mohandas K. Gandhi, *From Yeravda Mandir* (Ahmedabad: Navajivan Publishing House, 1945), pp. 53-54.
3. Quoted in Bose, *Selections from Gandhi,* p. 42.

5

EXPLORATIONS IN GANDHI'S THEORY OF NONVIOLENCE

Karl H. Potter

> "Hope for the future" I have never lost and never will, because it is embedded in my undying faith in non-violence. What has, however, clearly happened in my case is the discovery that in all probability there is a vital defect in my technique of the working of non-violence. . . . Failure of my technique of non-violence causes no loss of faith in non-violence itself. On the contrary, that faith is, if possible, strengthened by the discovery of a possible flaw in the technique.[1]

With these poignant sentiments, penned less than a year before his death, Gandhi expresses his unhappiness at the communal violence which had flared up upon the achievement of *swaraj*, independence for India. Characteristically, he faults his own contribution rather than casting blame at those instigating the conflict, though this self-castigation needs to be understood as a part of a continuing process by which Gandhi shamed his people into living up to his standards. These standards are, clearly enough, extremely high. A less demanding leader, enjoying the fruits of the successful application of techniques which he invented and promulgated, would not criticize those techniques merely because they did not solve all the world's problems at a single stroke. Yet Gandhi finds a "flaw" in those very techniques which were centrally involved in one of the most remarkable political upheavals in history.

The phrase Gandhi uses in the quotation offered above—"flaw in the technique"—indicates that he thought that the failure of the method lay in the way the theory of nonviolence was applied. I take it that when he affirms his faith in nonviolence, while noting the "flaw in the technique," he supposes that the principle is unquestionable, the application of it open to question. But this analysis is not the only one that might be made, and it should be compared with others which attribute the failure to different sources. It may be, after all, that Gandhi's expectations are wholly unrealistic, that both the theory of nonviolence and its application in India's case were unexceptional. Perhaps, in assessing the results, a typical idealistic mistake was committed, that of failing to take into consideration the frailty of human beings. Gandhi is himself frequently mindful of this possibility in his writings and speeches; he points out that violence is a relative matter, relative to the station of the agent as well as to the times in which he lives.[2] It would seem consistent with these remarks to speak of the inconstancy of human nature rather than of a flaw in technique.

This is not the point of view, however, that I wish to take in beginning the present paper. Though it is evident that human nature is frail and productive of our miseries, merely to say so produces no improvements. Let us, then, note another way that Gandhi's analysis of the supposed failure may have gone wrong. Perhaps, the trouble is in the theory, not in the technique. That is to say, perhaps some of the assumptions underlying the Gandhian notion of nonviolence are faulty; while what was done in India was a perfectly sound application of Gandhi's principles, the principles themselves need reexamination. To be sure, it is difficult to draw any sharp demarcation between theory and practice in this instance—the theory of nonviolent resistance is, in fact, the technique of its application. Nevertheless, I hope to suggest that questions may be asked about some of Gandhi's general pronouncements concerning nonviolence. It is at least conceivable that by examining in a critical way some of his notions about what nonviolence is, we may pave the way toward constructive efforts to develop a consistent theory of nonviolence. I put forth this possibility as one which Gandhi himself would have been likely to explore, for I think that when he speaks of techniques, he really intends to include some, if not all, of the theoretical considerations I shall be speaking about. In a frank and open search for truth, one must examine all hypotheses with equal care, and, despite the veneration with which Gandhi is held, it would be unfortunate if respect for the man were to function as an impediment to a fuller understanding of his contribution.

The basic operative assumption which Gandhi makes is that nonviolence constitutes a positive procedure for promoting worthwhile social change. It is not merely that we should refrain from violence because it is wrong. Sometimes violence is not wrong; there are conditions in which one is justified in inflicting violence, e.g., when one is confronted with a choice between doing so and acting in a cowardly manner.[3] Thus, the question is not one of establishing on philosophical grounds the absolute disvalue of violence and, therefrom, the absolute value of nonviolence. The theory of nonviolence is not a system of moral philosophy or even part of a system. Rather, it is an aspect of what is sometimes called casuistry, the science of discovering what to do upon specific occasions. To indicate the conditions under which nonviolent resistance may be practiced is not a matter of deciding when it is expedient to embark on a program whose moral worth is generically justified on some other grounds. Rather, the conditions under which nonviolence can operate are precisely the crux of the theory of nonviolence, setting limits to the very notion of what nonviolence is. In coming to understand the meaning of nonviolence, then, we should begin by cataloguing the conditions under which, as Gandhi sees it, nonviolence can or cannot occur.

As is frequently the case, it is easier to give negative conditions than positive ones. Rather than list all the possible situations in which nonviolence is practicable, we can more easily mention a number of occurrences which Gandhi says render nonviolence impracticable or impossible. We may divide these conditions into three major sorts. First, there are conditions in the environment, types of external circumstances, which render nonviolent techniques inadvisable or unworkable or unlikely to succeed. Secondly, there are conditions in the agents who propose to adopt nonviolent procedures which will preclude their success or which will even make it impossible to designate their behavior as nonviolent. Third, there are conditions in the method of the agents which will defeat the purpose of nonviolence or which will make the term nonviolence inapplicable.

Gandhi spoke of several environmental conditions which, by their very existence, render nonviolence impossible. The first is so obvious that it is not easy to cite any specific reference in Gandhi's writings for it, but, nevertheless, it is clearly assumed by him to have this force. If the type of change that is contemplated is believed by the agent to be one which leads to a state less beneficial than the present one, the methods used to bring about this change can hardly be described as nonviolent. Suppose that I plan to resist a law which I believe to be just by refusing to obey that law, a method of resistance which I describe as nonviolent. Gandhi would not allow that my method is really nonviolent despite its being a type of behavior which might constitute nonviolent resistance were the law in question thought by me to be unjust. The principles behind this are, I take it, that obedience to just laws leads (other things being equal) to more beneficial states of society whereas disobedience to such laws leads to less beneficial states, and that actions are not nonviolent unless they are intended to lead to more beneficial states or, at any rate, to maintain the present level of justice.

Nonviolent resistance is also precluded unless the resistance is undertaken as a response to an instance of violence.

It should also be remembered that nonviolence comes into play only when it comes into contact with violence. One who refrains from violence when there is no occasion for its exercise is simply un-violent and has no credit for his inaction.[4]

It is difficult to know just what this condition involves until we have some idea of what Gandhi accounts as violence. This underlines the need for an examination of his ideas on that matter.[5] I shall examine the subject later.

The lack of a "true and substantial issue" is another environmental condition which Gandhi felt precluded the use of nonviolence. This is referred to in a passage in which he specifically lists "conditions necessary for the success of Satyagraha" and includes among them, "the issue must be true and substantial."[6] It is difficult to see how one goes about distinguishing "true and substantial" issues from those that cannot be so characterized. Is the distinction to be drawn in terms of the strength of the commitment by the parties concerned, the amount of good or harm the parties expect or fear from the actions they contemplate, or the amount of good or harm which will, in fact, accrue from these actions? One is reminded of the considerations invoked by Jeremy Bentham in his "hedonistic calculus" whereby one was supposed to be able to calculate the moral worth of a deed by weighing amounts falling into a number of categories.

Perhaps Gandhi, in mentioning such a requirement, has something else in mind, namely that the success of satyagraha depends in part on the accompanying publicity through which the purveyor of violence is publicly shamed and thus induced to reconsider his actions. In that case, however, successful satyagraha does not of necessity demand a "true and substantial" issue, unless Gandhi wishes to disallow private bravery as not qualifying at all. If you and I are alone, and you threaten me with violence, and I resist you by defensive tactics coupled with a running commentary appealing to your higher instincts, I practice nonviolent resistance even though, by subsequent agreement, neither of us alludes to the incident again. It seems to me that even if your threats of violence are occasioned by childish concerns, so that no "true and substantial" issue is discernible in our dispute, I have, nevertheless, practiced nonviolent resistance.

The second major category of conditions which will preclude the use of nonviolence involves elements in the agents. The first and foremost of these conditions, judging by the frequency with which Gandhi returns to the point, is cowardice. "Cowardice," he writes, "is wholly inconsistent with non-violence."[7] Although Gandhi elsewhere speaks of grades of nonviolence which are determined by the moral fibre of the agents, and includes the nonviolence of the coward (as well as of the brave and the weak),[8] by his own definition nonviolence of the coward is a misnomer. It cannot exist. If the situation really is one where the only available alternatives are violence or cowardice, nonviolent methods are altogether precluded by the nature of the external situation. But action is not precluded. This point is emphasized by Gandhi's statement that where the choice is between violence and cowardice, one should choose violence.

> I do believe that, where there is only a choice between cowardice and violence, I would advise violence. Thus when my eldest son asked me what he should have done, had he been present when I was almost fatally assaulted in 1908, whether he should have run away and seen me killed or whether he should have used his physical force which he could and wanted to use, and defended me, I told him that it was his duty to defend me even by using violence. . . .

> But I believe that non-violence is infinitely superior to violence, forgiveness is more manly than punishment. Forgiveness adorns a soldier. But abstinence is forgiveness only when there is power to punish; it is meaningless when it pretends to proceed from a helpless creature. A mouse hardly forgives a cat when it allows itself to be torn to pieces by her. . . .[9]

We can understand from this passage that Gandhi would not allow that cowardly compliance to the tyrant's sword constituted nonviolence; at least it is not the sort of nonviolence which he intended to teach Indians who sought *swaraj*. One must not be a coward who turns and runs when threatened with violence. At the same time, the requirements for a successful satyagrahi include his willingness "to suffer till the end."[10] While presumably Gandhi would be unwilling to say that a person who succumbed to torture, after enduring a great deal of pain for a considerable period, no longer deserved the name of satyagrahi, it remains true that in distinguishing between the weak and the strong, Gandhi proceeds in such a manner that most of us, having a breaking-point despite our high resolve and being unable to suffer until the end, would have to be adjudged weak in comparison with Gandhi's ideals of strength.

These severe strictures are softened by Gandhi's compassionate view of human nature as well as by his willingness to admit differences among the capacities of individuals. Gandhi was no absolute moralist.

> What is one man's food can be another's poison. Meat-eating is a sin for me. Yet, for another person, who has always lived on meat and never seen anything wrong in it, to give it up simply in order to copy me will be a sin. . . . Evil and good are relative terms. . . .[11]

Gandhi's teachings about nonviolence should not be construed as if they were meant to be elements in a system of moral philosophy but rather as guiding principles in casuistry. Much of Gandhi's writing is unfortunately taken up with answers to tiresome tweakings by critics who seek to show, for example, that Gandhi ought to refrain from killing snakes or monkeys if he is to be consistent. Since Gandhi was not a philosopher undertaking to develop an overall theory of morality, they are beside the point. Gandhi does not suppose that what is right for *x* need be so for *y*. He does not suppose, furthermore, that he knows for sure how to tell what is right for anyone.

In the light of his sublime humility, then, we may construe

Gandhi's remarks on the distinction between strong and weak nonviolence as hortatory rather than descriptive. The best satyagrahi is he who can last the course. Others may be satyagrahis to the limits of their abilities. Indeed, India's freedom may well have depended as much on the impact of the numbers of weaker resisters as on the steadfast resolve of the stronger.

Another condition which, if it exists in the satyagrahi, will preclude his acting nonviolently is a lack of self-respect, a tendency to act from expediency rather than from principle. Writing in *Young India* in 1926, Gandhi quotes a letter describing a party quarrel in which members of one party visited various indignities upon members of another. The writer wished him to state whether nonviolence required that one suffer such insulting treatment. Gandhi replies:

> I can only congratulate those who are spat upon, or assaulted, or had night-soil thrown upon them. No injury has happened to them, if they had the courage to suffer the insult without even mental retaliation. But it was wholly wrong on their part to suffer it, if they felt irritated but refrained out of expedience from retaliating. A sense of self-respect disdains all expedience.[12]

Gandhi goes on to speculate as to what sort of nonviolent response might be appropriate by way of resistance. It is clear that in this case Gandhi views the indignities as constituting violence; he believes, therefore, that nonviolent resistance is appropriate and desirable and that passivity, while conceivably a type of nonviolent resistance, can not be termed such if it issues from anything but principle. Only if the self-respect of those assaulted dictated ignoring the insults as constituting the most appropriate method of retaliation would such inaction count as nonviolence.

This is an appeal for a kind of wisdom on the part of the satyagrahi which is considerably more than mere courage. It requires a rather mature and sophisticated person not to lose his head in such circumstances, for there is the temptation either to react with passion or to fail to react at all out of what Gandhi calls here "expedience." The kind of wisdom involved is akin to that required of a wise parent in dealing with his child's irritating behavior, and parents are all too aware of their inability to discover the appropriate response in more than a few of the instances calling for such wisdom.

The extreme importance assigned by Gandhi to the inward aspects of nonviolence sharpens into focus as we consider the third internal condition of the agent which will preclude nonviolence.

> It is of course assumed that the outward act is an expression of the inward intention. One who having retaliation in his breast submits to violence out of policy is not truly non-violent, and may even be a hypocrite if he hides his intention.[13]

And again:

> A devotee of Truth may not do anything in deference to convention. He must always hold himself open to correction, and whenever he discovers himself to be wrong he must confess it at all cost and atone for it.[14]

Gandhi avers over and over again that nonviolence and truth are but two sides of the same coin, the coin of *anāsaktiyoga*.[15] The nonviolent resister must be honest with himself and others. A hypocrite cannot be nonviolent, and one who restrains his anger ("having retaliation in his breast") and adopts a policy of passivity which does not reflect his true feelings is not to be described as nonviolent. Again, we shall do well to take this characterization of nonviolent resisters of the brave variety as the ideal. For there is no doubt, it seems to me, that most of those who participate in nonviolent resistance are not free from anger toward their adversaries but feel that checking this emotion, sublimating it, perhaps, by adopting nonviolent means, will be more constructive and efficacious.

Gandhi, however, insists that the mere existence in the agent of violent feelings prevents successful satyagraha. "The Satyagrahi," he says, "should not have any hatred in his heart against the opponent."[16] It is required that the person or persons against whom the resistance is practiced must be able to recognize in the agent the pure motives which move him to practice nonviolent resistance.

> Non-violent resistance can only follow some real disinterested service, some heart-expression of love. For instance, I would have no status to resist a savage offering animal sacrifice until he could recognize in me his friend through some loving act of mine or other means.[17]

In these words, written in 1928, Gandhi sought to justify his participation in the First World War, for the reason that "though as an individual I was opposed to war, I had no status for offering effective non-violent resistance."[18]

Gandhi frequently equates ahimsa, nonviolence, with love, and it is not surprising that he here argues, in effect, that where the conditions for love are not present, nonviolence cannot be present. However, this is a principle not easily applied. It is all too tempting to suppose that violence is more commonly justified than Gandhi allowed, on the basis that the evil in one's opponent has made him incapable of recognizing one's love for him. Thus, one is left with no alternative except violence or cowardice, in which case, as we have seen, Gandhi would advocate violence.

Clearly it will not do to take one's disapproval of another as a sufficient reason for judging him an amoral monster. What does constitute a sufficient reason for such a judgment, then? Remember that Gandhi seems to suggest that he had no way in the circumstances of the First World War to convey his love to those prosecuting the conflict, and he proffers an analogy which would seem, in the context, to suggest that it was their blindness, not his inability, which was responsible for this failure of communication. Why should he have assumed that they were blind in this way? We may find a way of explaining this subsequently.

A more recent episode also illustrates Gandhi's belief that the heart of the resister must not be hardened with hatred. A Negro couple visited Gandhi, and the lady posed to him the question: "How am I to act, supposing my own brother was lynched before my very eyes?" Gandhi's answer was: "I must not wish ill to these, but neither must I cooperate with them."[19] And he went on to advise a fast, "an act of self-immolation," as an appropriate response to the situation. The world has begun to appreciate the sagacity of Gandhi's counsel, but I venture to say that even those who might consider such measures would be very dubious about their ability to avoid experiencing antipathy toward the lynchers. Yet Gandhi speaks as if such saintliness were not only desirable but requisite in order for a technique to be worthy of the designation nonviolent.

The final inward characteristic of the agent which will prevent his acting in a genuinely nonviolent manner is his inability to act violently. Gandhi writes: "Man for man the strength of non-violence is in exact proportion to the ability, not the will, of the non-violent person to inflict violence."[20] In another place, he says: "Non-violence, therefore, presupposes the ability to strike."[21] It would seem from this that the resister must have it in his power to inflict violence of a sort comparable to the effect that his nonviolent action may have.

It is worth noting that this sentiment is in general agreement with that expressed by Krishna in the Bhagavad-Gita, the Hindu classic which Gandhi so revered. In the second part of the Gita, Krishna appeals to Arjuna to practice an attitude of nonattachment (*vairāgya*, equal to Gandhi's *anāsakti*), at the same time using his caste-determined abilities as a basis for the discipline. Specifically, Krishna advises Arjuna to fight in the Mahabharata war but to do so in the spirit of nonattachment.[22] Here is a soldier whose dharma is to participate in battle: he should practice nonviolence, not inaction, and "the strength of [his] nonviolence is in exact proportion to [his] ability to inflict violence."

But what would such a soldier do by way of practicing nonviolence? To answer this, we need to know what constitutes violence. It is clear, however, that Gandhi does not think the soldier can fight and at the same time act nonviolently. To this extent, his thinking departs dramatically from that of Krishna, who seems to think that fighting is quite compatible with *anāsaktiyoga*, the discipline of nonattachment.

What is the nub of the difference between Gandhi's and Krishna's thinking here? They both agree, it seems, that to be nonattached a soldier must have the ability to be violent; they disagree as to whether participation in war might be counted as nonattached action. Gandhi attempts to deny the discrepancy by arguing that what is accounted as violence has changed since the time of the Mahabharata.

> Many things which we look upon as non-violent will, perhaps, be considered violent by future generations. For, we destroy life when we use milk or cereals as food. Therefore, it is quite possible that posterity will give up milk production and the cultivation of food-grains. Just as we consider ourselves as non-violent in spite of our consumption of milk and food-grains, so also in the age of the *Gītā* fighting was such a common thing that no one thought it was contrary to *Ahimsā*.[23]

Thus, while fighting might be properly cited by Krishna as a method of nonattached action, it cannot be so cited by Gandhi, since it is opposed to nonviolence. But we still do not understand precisely why, for we have not as yet studied what Gandhi means by violence.

Returning, however, to the requirement that "non-violence presupposes ability to strike," one sympathizes with the following question posed by "a London Friend":

> Is not non-violent resistance by the militarily strong more effective than that by the militarily weak?

Gandhi answers, in part:

> This is a contradiction in terms. There can be no non-violence
> offered by the militarily strong. Thus, Russia in order to express
> her non-violence has to discard all her power of doing violence.
> What is true is that if these, who were at one time strong in
> armed might, change their mind, they will be better able to
> demonstrate their non-violence to the world and, therefore,
> also to their opponents. . . . [24]

But if so, this constitutes an *ad hoc* exception to the general
principle behind the requirement here under discussion. If "the
strength of non-violence is in exact proportion to the ability, not
the will, of the non-violent person to inflict violence," then it
cannot be a contradiction in terms that nonviolent resistance by
the militarily strong is more effective than that by the militarily
weak. One thus comes to the conclusion that war constitutes a
special case for Gandhi, a context to which advice applicable
elsewhere fails to apply. I think this can be evidenced decisively
by careful scrutiny of other passages, but this would be beyond
what I can attempt here.

The third and last type of condition which will preclude
nonviolence, according to Gandhi, is to be found in the methods
of the agents of nonviolent resistance. We may consider these
more briefly, not because they are less important, but because
they do not help us much more in understanding nonviolence than
we are helped by appreciating the foregoing conditions. First, if
the methods of the agent involve secrecy, they do not meet the
requirements of nonviolence. Gandhi seems to have connected this
condition with the general point about truth and its relation to
nonviolence. Presumably, a part of the reason for excluding secre-
tive methods is that, given protection, a method may easily become the object of dogmatism and be espoused in such a way
as to disallow criticism and self-correction. The virtues of techniques which are open to constant critical appraisal are obvious,
and that they are close to the center of the spirit of nonviolence

has been well brought out by others, most recently by Horsburgh.[25]

By the same token, where the method chosen precludes the resistee's learning to change his attitude, the aims of nonviolent resistance cannot be achieved. Gandhi frequently points out that the purpose of nonviolent resistance methods is to produce a change of heart in the opponent, and if the method chosen is, for one of several reasons, likely to result in hardening of the resistee's attitudes, the method is not to be thought of as nonviolent.

Where the method involves more violence than is necessary, it is not properly called nonviolent. Violence, Gandhi notes, is more or less unavoidable in life as we live it from day to day, but one can try to minimize it by choosing among possible responses to situations in appropriate ways. A specific application of this point occurs when one proposes to coerce another, even if the coercion is intended to stop the coerced person from violence. Thus, asked if one should provide fish for fish-eaters, Gandhi responds: "The man who coerces another not to eat fish commits more violence than he who eats it. . . . The man who uses coercion is guilty of deliberate violence. Coercion is inhuman. . . ."[26] Just how to decide what is coercion and what is not is another matter. Presumably, if we understand how Gandhi uses the term violence, we may be able to guess how he understands coercion and vice versa.

Moreover, where the method itself produces (rather than involves) more injustice than existed previously, it is not a nonviolent method. The most obvious example of a kind of method which has this propensity is war, armed conflict. At least, so Gandhi seems to assume. But again, we need to understand how he defines violence to see clearly why war is always considered productive of worse consequences than any other action.

To summarize what I believe may be gleaned from this review of Gandhi's thoughts on the conditions precluding violence, I mention the following points. A good many actions which others might construe as nonviolent will not be counted so by Gandhi, if we take his strictures seriously. However, although we can detail Gandhi's reasons for not considering an action nonviolent, it is difficult to see an overall principle behind them. There are reasons for this. First, Gandhi is not offering a moral theory; his remarks are always fashioned in connection with concrete cases, and he follows his intuitions in deciding whether a given action has the marks of nonviolence. Thus, we should not expect consistency and theoretical completeness from him. Furthermore, Gandhi offers no formal definition of violence although many of his conditions for being nonviolent are conditions which can be understood only if one can presuppose an ability to distinguish what is violent from what is not. He explicitly endorses a thorough-going relativism about what counts as violence—what is violent for x may not be for y, what was violent then may not be now or vice versa.

It should also be noted that Gandhi moves far too easily between internal and external factors when discussing the components of nonviolence. He appears to make the assumption that the nonviolence of an action depends on, and is the inevitable consequence of, high moral character in the agent. One result of this is to compromise the term nonviolent in describing either action or agent. Some actions that we would be inclined to call nonviolent are excluded by Gandhi's insistence on moral qualities in the agent which may well not be present. And conversely, an agent whose character traits include love, truthfulness, and courage, whose attitudes are, therefore, appropriately described as nonviolent as Gandhi uses the term, may well undertake actions, which, however admirable their motivation, are deemed by experts as productive of more violence rather than less.

Finally, we have seen that in treating one major type of action, namely war, Gandhi appears to invoke an absolutist code which precludes participating in war altogether, regardless of whether such action appears to satisfy all the other requirements. This flies in the face of his procedures in treating other types of decision as to how to act.

It cannot be claimed that Gandhi is guilty of promulgating an inconsistent moral theory, if only because he is proposing no moral theory whatsoever. Nevertheless, the vagueness and tensions in his thought, alluded to in the foregoing summary, may suggest the possibility mentioned at the outset, namely, that there is still room for improvement in his theory of nonviolence. Gandhi's dissatisfaction may have been due not so much to a defect in the applications of the method as to his understanding of the principles underlying the method. Improvements in this theory, it would seem, might stem from clarification of key terms such as violence. In the remainder of this paper, I am going to explore possible explications of the distinction between violence and nonviolence as Gandhi and others have discussed these terms.

How the distinction between violence and nonviolence is drawn depends, among other things, on whether one is operating under Western or classical Indian assumptions. Gandhi, I suggest, thinks of nonviolence as closely bound up with nonattachment in the Indian context. Difficulties are created when he brings in Western problems and tries to apply the notion to them. Sometimes the theory is so foreign to the problems that the application is obscure; on other occasions, as in the case of war, the application violates Gandhi's intuitions of what nonattachmen ought to involve. Gandhi's problem is how to draw the line between violence and nonviolence so as to include in the latter just those attitudes and actions he believes consonant with morality, taking his cue largely from classical Indian self-realizational moral theory. Perhaps, to state my central contention for what it is worth, Gandhi's program depends on an accurate understanding of the principles of classical Indian theory of value; to the extent to which his understanding was vague or erroneous, to that extent the theory of nonviolence suffers from the same shortcomings. That Gandhi might, if he were here, be nodding his agreement is suggested by the following:

> Man is not to drown himself in the well of shastras but he is to dive in their broad ocean and bring out pearls. At every

step he has to use his discrimination as to what is ahimsa and what is himsa. In this there is no room for shame or cowardice. . . . [27]

It is very difficult to find a definition of violence in Gandhi's writings. The best I have been able to come up with is this: " 'Himsa' means causing pain or killing any life out of anger, or from a selfish purpose, or with the intention of injuring it."[28] It is worth comparing this meaning with Webster's latest attempts at defining violence:

> Exertion of any physical force so as to injure or abuse (as in warfare or in effecting an entrance into a house); . . . injury in the form of revoking, repudiation, distortion, infringement, or irreverence to a thing, nation, or quality fitly valued or observed; . . . intense, turbulent or furious action, force, or feeling, often destructive. . . . [29]

A noticeable contrast between Gandhi and Webster is that Gandhi takes violence to be a matter of the agent's feelings and intentions, whereas Webster takes it to be a matter of behaviour and its results. Webster, apparently, considers warfare to be violent because it involves exertion of physical force which in fact injures or abuses, while Gandhi considers warfare to be violent because of the attitudes with which human beings enter into it. Webster's definition is inadequate for Gandhi's purposes, since it fails to capture the internal feature of violence which Gandhi finds essential. On the other hand, Gandhi's own definition is inadequate as well, for it is not evident that a person must undertake warfare "out of anger, or from a selfish purpose, or with the intention of injuring [life]." As we have noted, Krishna seems to have advised Arjuna to undertake warfare with none of these attitudes or intentions. What Gandhi needs by way of definition, it would seem, is a statement which brings together the internal and external aspects of violence by explaining or justifying his notion that the moral character of the act is conditioned by the moral character of the agent. Gandhi must persuade us that the feelings and intentions of the agent are as relevant to the morality of the act as he thinks they are.

Newton Garver has pointed out that:

> Violence often involves physical force, and the association of force with violence is very close: in many contexts the words become synonyms. . . . But in human affairs violence and force cannot be equated. Force without violence is often used on a person's body. If a man is in the throes of drowning, the standard Red Cross life-saving techniques specify force which is certainly not violence. To equate an act of rescue with an act of violence would be to lose sight entirely of the significance of the concept. . . . Violence in human affairs is much more closely connected with the idea of violation than with the idea of force. What is fundamental about violence is that a person is violated.[30]

Garver proceeds to explain that this characteristic use of the term violence implies certain assumptions on our part about "fundamental natural rights of persons." These include, he claims, "a right to his body, to determine what his body does and what is done to his body . . ." and "the right to autonomy" which requires others to respect the dignity of a person, "his ability to make his own decisions."

This seems an attractive suggestion to follow out, for it holds promise of providing the explanation or justification that we are seeking, one which will show that the internal and external aspects of violence spring fundamentally from the same source. An act is violent when there is intent on the part of the agent to violate others. When there is no such intent, a piece of behavior which in fact injures others is not violent, although it may be culpable in that the agent could and should have seen to it that it did not occur. Nonviolence, then, will be just that disposition on the part of an agent which systematically avoids intentionally violating others, and nonviolent action is that type of act which is executed by a nonviolent agent.

What, though, does "violating others" involve? Garver thinks a person's body is fundamental to his being a person.

> A person has certain rights which are undeniably, indissolubly, connected with his being a person. One of these is a right to his body, to determine what his body does and what is done to his body—inalienable because without his body he would cease to be a person.[31]

Presumably, depriving another of his body is necessarily to violate him, since without a body he cannot very well determine what his body does and what is done to it.

But one can easily bring this line of thinking into question. For one thing, what of someone who determines that he wishes his body to be destroyed? Is it violation, and thus violence, to do away with one's own body? Suppose I restrain someone from committing suicide—am I violating him? I would think that to be consistent Garver should take it that I am violating him. Suppose, to drive the point home even more firmly, that A freely determines that he wishes B to put him to death (let us say that A is a martyr for a worthy cause), and B does so. Has B violated A? He has, in a sense, deprived A of the right to determine what his body does, but this is paradoxical, since B has acted to effect what A determined that his body should do.

The implications are not confined to extreme or bizarre cases. The state deprives an individual of his right to determine what his body does when it imprisons him for a crime. Is the state then guilty of violent action—does it violate the criminal by punishing him in this way?

Garver applies his own analysis of violence to a number of cases, in the course of which he generalizes: "Whenever you employ force on another person's body without his consent you are attacking not just a physical entity but a person—and that is personal overt violence."[32] Garver goes on immediately to the conclusion that warfare is violence. But this is questionable, even on his own assumptions. For is it not sometimes the case that the various parties in a war, by the very fact of their participation, are, in effect, giving their consent? To be sure, an aggressor who attacks another with the intent of depriving him of his body or his autonomy may be said to violate him, since the attacked party presumably does not give his consent—but how about the response? If A avails himself of violence in attacking B, is not this tacitly to give consent to B to reply by use of force? And further, if B does reply with a use of force, can we really say that he violates A? If we can, it seems to me we must have in mind some principle other than the ones Garver provides. For it is not clear that B, in responding with force to an aggressor, is employing force on another's body without his consent, nor does it seem clear that he is either depriving him of his right to autonomy or affronting his dignity. Indeed, the natural moral training of a Western child works directly against such an assumption. What is undignified is to refrain from returning force when violently assaulted, and someone who, even nonviolently, restrains an American boy from retaliating when he is punched in the eye, is, in the morality of the everyday world, depriving that boy of his right to autonomy, his dignity and the right to choose what he should do with his body.

The Indian tradition is different in this respect, I should judge, though probably the morality of the everyday world is the same everywhere. In Indian classical thought no such emphasis was placed on the body as crucial to a person's being what he is. Indeed, the root of bondage is frequently held to be located in the tendency to equate one's person with one's body. It is thus not *ipso facto* an instance of violating a person to deprive him of his body, and this fact may help considerably in appreciating Gandhi's notions about the Gita. Arjuna, trained in the high classical morality, is not concerned about depriving his kinsfolk of life and limb; his concerns are clearly seen to be centered around his fear of producing "mixture of caste" (*jātisamgraha*). This concern certainly features a conception of human dignity and may have to do with his kinsfolk's right to autonomy, although the autonomy in question is not perhaps to be spelled out in precisely the terms Garver uses. And Krishna's advice is addressed to Arjuna, not to the American schoolboy; he emphasizes that Arjuna's dignity lies in performing his dharma well, and this involves killing his kinsfolk. Gandhi notes that our ideas of violence have changed since Arjuna's time. Perhaps the change is precisely that we now count a person's body as a fundamental aspect of his person where before we did not, so that all use of force against a person's body constitutes violation, thus violence.

But Gandhi has not made this out. For even though it may well be that nowadays Indians, as well as Americans, construe their person as inalienably involving their particular body, it does not at all follow that they normally take every use of force against a body as constituting violation of a person. Force, when used against one with one's consent, may be painful and even deadly, but it is not generally held to be violation of the person. Garver writes: "In war, what one army tries to inflict on another is what happens to individuals in cases of mugging and murder."[33] But that is not really so, since in the case of mugging or murder one person injures another without his consent, while in cases of war—or at least in some cases of war, for the term covers many different kinds of conflict—the parties injure each other with each other's consent.

Thus, if Gandhi's sweeping characterization of warfare as constituting violence is to be justified, it cannot be justified merely on the ground that people nowadays generally take all threats to life and limb as constituting violation of a person, for they do not. Nor will it do to try to trace the notion to classical Hindu thought, for we have seen in the example of the Gita (and it could be evidenced further), Gandhi himself admits that people in those days had a different notion of violence, one that allowed warfare as nonviolation.

It appears, and Gandhi seems to appreciate this too, that if one is to define war as necessarily constituting violence one must show that it harms the agent who prosecutes war whether or not the other party consents. This suggests a fundamental reason why Gandhi dwells predominantly on the inner aspects of violence and nonviolence. Mulford Sibley has, I think, seen this and tried to incorporate it into an account of violence. Characterizing Hindu pacifism, he writes:

> Violence is the creation of a disturbance in the structure of that soul-substance which is the common heritage of all life. It is any act which tends to accentuate the separateness of one soul from another—and from the God to which souls are seeking to return—separateness which is to some degree inevitable within the realm of material incarnation but which has to be resisted.[34]

Likewise R. B. Gregg, without explicitly identifying this analysis with anything Hindu, writes:

> Violence is any act, motive, thought, active feeling, or outwardly directed attitude which is divisive in nature or results in respect to emotions or inner attitude; that is to say, inconsistent with spiritual unity.[35]

Does such analysis as these writers suggest fit better the spirit of Gandhi's notion of violence? Perhaps it does. But it is intolerably vague as it stands. We need to understand under what conditions a contemplated act is inconsistent with spiritual unity, and when there occurs a disturbance in the structure of the soul-substance. Furthermore, Gandhi did not, as a rule, appeal to any clarifications of why an act threatens the spirit when he rationalized his advice on practical matters. If he had, in fact, done so, one may well question whether we would nowadays revere Gandhi as the little man who moved millions. Though Gandhi's assumptions may have required that he give spiritual advice, individual by individual, as the classical gurus did, his situation and the frame of mind of those he addressed made that kind of advice impracticable and impertinent.

It should be clear at this point from our discussion of Gandhi's views on the characteristics of violence and nonviolence as distinguished from other definitions that an understanding of the depths of the human person is what is required to justify Gandhi's casuistry, if, indeed, it can be justified at all. This makes more remarkable the success of Gandhi's program. Somehow Gandhi evoked in those who followed him a faith of sorts, the faith that he saw more deeply into their souls than they themselves could. Men need the kind of confidence which they gain from following a leader in whom they have this kind of faith, and perhaps Gandhi's success is largely a matter of his being at the right place at the right time to provide it for them, despite the vagueness and confusion of his own thought. But there is another possibility, namely, that Gandhi, perhaps without fully realizing it, caught the spirit of a basis for moral philosophy which is universal, or at any rate close to the heart of both Indian and European philosophy, and that it was this aspect of his teaching which provided the basis for his following. If that is so, it seems safe to say that at the heart of Indian and European philosophy, there is something which may be roughly designated as self-realizationism, a view which makes the improvement of the individual person the fundamental task each of us should pursue. Gandhi's intuitions about what does and what does not conduce to enrichment of the self, though avowedly unsystematic, were respected and revered by those who followed him not so much because they believed his views were in every respect correct as because their direction was relevant to aims which the followers felt worthwhile.

This suggestion may help explain a good deal that has seemed puzzling in what has gone before in this paper. It makes eminently right Gandhi's high standards as a leader and his dissatisfaction with his program even in the midst of its success. The spirit of self-realizationism dictates vigilance and non-attachment especially at the times when pride and other temptations are most inviting. If the leader succumbs to these temptations and relaxes his vigilance, the program is undermined. *Swaraj* was but a stage on life's way for Gandhi, and it would have been inconsistent for him to act as if anything of permanence had been gained merely by arriving at this stage.

The suggestion that Gandhi's philosophy is unsystematic self-realizationism also makes plain why the most important conditions defining nonviolence must be internal ones. It is the realization of the self which matters, and so in some way or other all advice must be traced to considerations pertaining to the individual's search for freedom or the Good. Even many of those conditions precluding nonviolence which I detailed in the first part of this paper turn out to be, on reinspection, reflections of the inner requirements. For example, the requirement that secrecy be avoided is clearly related to the thesis that the realization of a self requires that self to remain always open-minded and receptive to criticism and new directions.

But what are we to say about Gandhi's thoughts on war? Why does he assume that participation in war is inevitably violent, that participation in armed conflict can under no circumstances assist one in self-realization? I do not think that he really can justify this assumption as it stands. But the possibility remains that he may be viewing war symbolically, as though the disintegration of society reflects the concomitant disintegration of the individuals connected with that society. This, however, brings in a different dimension, one I should think we would associate with Western thought rather more than with Hinduism, unless we are dealing with a variety of neo-Vedanta, where this kind of symbolic extension is a characteristic pattern of thought.

I conclude by once again addressing the questions raised in the opening paragraphs. Possibly there is a flaw in the technique, or even more probably, a flaw in the theory of nonviolence. Nonviolence—and this seems at first glance paradoxical—does not require us to refrain from causing pain or even death to others. On Gandhi's terms, even participation in war is not *ipso facto* violent. Violence is, from Gandhi's point of view, fundamentally an attitude on the part of the agent, and a man may participate in war as a soldier without the emotions which Gandhi identifies as constituting himsa: anger, selfishness, or other emotions inimical to self-realizational efforts. Indeed, such emotions are recognized as threats to the success of a military effort, and a soldier's training is directed to the end that he will be free from such passions. Gandhi's exaggerated, unconditional, and sweeping condemnation of participation in warfare is unjustifiable on his own terms, no matter how much we may sympathize with it. Thus, when he reflects that the strife of Hindu and Muslim proves a defect in the techniques of nonviolence, he should not conclude that the proof arises because all strife is violent, but rather because this particular conflict is. As a general matter, a given agent may well discipline himself to greater self-realization in the heat of battle. If a communal riot is not an arena where such self-realization activity can occur, it must be because of the nature of communal rioting, not just because it is warfare. If Gandhi insists that all war is violent, he must find other principles to show that this is so, principles he does not display and which would, I fear, run against many of his beliefs.

NOTES

1. Mohandas K. Gandhi, *Non-Violence in Peace and War* (Ahmedabad: Navajivan Publishing House, 1949), 2:336. This passage is quoted from *Harijan,* November 11, 1947.
2. Mohandas K. Gandhi, *The Teaching of the Gita,* ed. A. T. Hingorani (Bombay: Bharatiya Vidya Bhavan, 1962), p. 7.
3. Gandhi, *Non-Violence in Peace and War,* 1:1.
4. *Ibid.,* 1:99-100.
5. The problem involved here is relatively unexplored. Though Susanne Rudolph has conducted sensitive research into Gandhi's conception of courage (Susanne H. Rudolph, "The New Courage: An Essay on Gandhi's Psychology," *World*

Politics 16 [October 1963]:98-117), less has been done by way of explicating Gandhi's use of the term violence.

6. "The conditions necessary for the success of Satyāgraha are (1) The Satyagrahi should not have any hatred in his heart against the opponent. (2) The issue must be true and substantial. (3) The Satyagrahi must be prepared to suffer till the end." Gandhi, *Non-Violence in Peace and War*, 2:61.

7. *Ibid.*, 1:59.

8. *Young India,* November 4, 1926, p. 385; quoted in S. C. Gangal, *The Gandhian Way to World Peace* (Bombay: Vica and Cox, 1960), p. 75.

9. Gandhi, *Non-Violence in Peace and War*, 1:1.

10. *Ibid.*, 2:61.

11. *Ibid.*, 2:65.

12. *Ibid.*, 1:60.

13. *Ibid.*, 1:99.

14. Mohandas K. Gandhi, *An Autobiography: The Story of My Experiments with Truth* (Boston: Beacon Press, 1957), p. 350.

15. See R. D. Ranada, *The Bhagavadgita as a Philosophy of God-Realization* (Bombay: Bharatiya Vidya Bhavan, 1964), p. 125.

16. Gandhi, *Non-Violence in Peace and War*, 2:61.

17. *Ibid.*, 1:71.

18. *Ibid.*

19. *Ibid.*, 1:115.

20. *Ibid.*, 1:111.

21. *Ibid.*, 1:60.

22. I have argued elsewhere that this is the proper way to interpret the second chapter of the Bhagavad-Gita. See K. H. Potter, *Presuppositions of India's Philosophies* (Englewood Cliffs, N. J.: Prentice-Hall, 1963), pp. 15-19; also "Religion as Resistance to Resignation," in *Studies on Asia, 1965* (Lincoln: University of Nebraska Press, 1966), pp. 193-200.

23. Gandhi, *The Teaching of the Gita*, p. 7.

24. Gandhi, *Non-Violence in Peace and War*, 2:91.

25. See H. J. N. Horsburgh, "The Distinctiveness of Satyagraha," *Philosophy East and West* 19 (April 1969):171-180;

also Mulford Q. Sibley, *The Political Theories of Modern Pacificism* (New York: Pacifist Research Bureau, 1944).

26. Gandhi, *Non-Violence in Peace and War*, 2:65.
27. *Ibid.*, 2:69.
28. *Young India*, November 4, 1926, p. 385; quoted in Gangal, *The Gandhian Way*, p. 74.
29. *Webster's New International Dictionary*, 3rd ed., s.u. "violence."
30. Newton Garver, "What Violence Is," *The Nation*, June 24, 1968, p. 819.
31. *Ibid.*
32. *Ibid.*
33. *Ibid.*
34. Sibley, *The Political Theories*, p. 2.
35. R. B. Gregg, *The Power of Non-Violence* (Philadelphia: Lippincott, 1934), p. 263.

6

GANDHI AND INDIAN FOREIGN POLICY

Werner Levi

On occasion, particularly on patriotic occasions, Indian speakers freely refer to the Mahatma as the great inspirer of India's international behavior. Yet, treatises dealing with Indian foreign policy have remarkably little to say about Gandhi's influence either upon the roots or the actual nature of the country's foreign relations. During his lifetime he had no major impact on Congress thinking about external affairs other than the question of British imperialism. Moreover, his death came at a moment when independent India's foreign policy was beginning to be shaped.

The most fundamental goals of a state—its survival as a political, territorial and cultural entity, the preservation of its national interest—are determined by the international political system. The weaker a nation, the narrower become the limits of the policy maker's decisions and the smaller becomes the possibility of expressing personal idiosyncrasies in foreign policy. As nationalists, Gandhi and his followers had to accept the major features of the international system, including the predominant role of power, the competition for the instruments of power and the relegation of morality to a minor position. Their attempts to attenuate the undesirable consequences of the nation-state system, for instance by redefining or qualifying nationalism or banning alliances, could only affect details of the system. The system itself prevented the significant influence of any ideology other than nationalism upon its functioning. This equalizing power of the international political system was strikingly demonstrated by the many new states entering the system after World War II. Most of them joined with the resolve to reform, if not revolutionize, the system's main features. India was a conspicuous leader of this group. But since they were all motivated by nationalism and the demand for sovereignity—the emotional and organizational basis of the system—they all, within a very short time, adjusted to the system which seemed so readily to respond to their dreams of absolute independence. The new nations exploited the system for their own purposes.[1]

A nation's foreign policy is affected not only by this international system but also by certain internal conditions. The material resources and geographic position of a country contribute to the formulation of its foreign policy as do the less easily traced factors of the people's physical and psychological capabilities. The stamina or unity of a people can spell the success or failure of a policy. There is, moreover, the political climate of a nation with which foreign policy must be compatible. One aspect of Gandhi's leadership lay in his recognition of and adjustment to these imponderable conditions, his awareness of the interaction between the political climate in which he operated and his own conduct. Though Gandhi succeeded at times in shaping political reality, he was very often also forced to adjust to it, to permit a compromise with his ideals, especially in the international realm.

Gandhi's death came before India's foreign policy had been defined. The influence of the ideology of a national hero like Gandhi tends to diminish when the hero is no longer present to agitate for the application of his values to specific situations and decisions. His ideas become, gradually, a part of the nation's ideological heritage. Their precision and distinctiveness become blunted by their integration into traditional and possibly contradictory beliefs. The national ideology must appear internally consistent in order to remain effective as a guide for social action and social control. Kautilya, Asoka, Gandhi and many others made their contributions to the formation of the ideology from which Indian society draws its guidance. Assertions by Indian writers or politicians that certain, usually virtuous, aspects of Indian foreign policy stem directly from Gandhi's ideas are either political tricks or pious exercises. We cannot trace directly Gandhi's impact on the character of foreign policy, but we can place Gandhi, the nationalist and moral teacher, into the perspective of the multiple determinants of India's foreign policy. To do this we must establish Gandhi's views on foreign policy issues, or in many cases his implied or likely views, and then examine the extent to which they correlate with actual Indian policies.

But even this approach fails to solve a problem arising from the inherent nature of any ideology. The values and beliefs of an ideology are always stated in broad, general terms. Such generality is a necessity since the function of an ideology is to guide behavior in a multitude of unforeseeable situations. The most likely applicable value or belief has to be selected, consciously or subconsciously, and interpreted to discover whether it applies to the given situation and what action or behavior it postulates. The selection as well as the interpretation is a largely subjective matter as is the perception of the situation. Different individuals— even those subscribing to the same general ideology—can reach very different conclusions regarding the acceptable or desirable action. When Gandhi makes such sweeping concepts as Truth, Cowardice, and Justice criteria for one or another kind of national behavior, there can be a vast divergency of opinion about the appropriateness of a foreign policy decision. Many different, even dichotomous decisions can be made, and actions undertaken, in the name of the same ideology. President McKinley decided to annex the Philippines on humanitarian grounds against the dictates of anti-colonialism. Yet, in the abstract, humanitarianism and anti-colonialism were compatible elements of the American national ideology. During the First World War, Gandhi offered his services to the British government, explaining to his people that such support was deserving by the Empire and might be to India's advantage. Only a few years earlier he had justified India's struggle against Great Britain with different elements of his ideology as the struggle between the "God of Love" and the "God of War."[2]

A very careful study of Gandhi's thoughts, more careful than is ever likely to be undertaken by a statesmen in public life, indicates, however, that what appear as contradictions are not necessarily such. Rather, they may be different conclusions from higher premises. When, for instance, Gandhi argues that nonviolent non-cooperation should not use obstruction if it forces the opponent into the moral dilemma of having to react in one of several immoral ways, he does not really allow any exception to the principles of nonviolent non-cooperation. He simply makes their application dependent upon the higher value of not putting a person into a moral dilemma. Such refinements, such careful hierarchial ordering of values, are not easily discerned, and even less easily heeded, in the application of moral principles to public social behavior.

Gandhi the activist and leader par excellence was aware of this difficulty. He was not greatly disturbed by actual inconsistencies. His aim, as he admitted frankly, "was not to be consistent with my previous statements on a given question, but to be consistent with the truth as it may present itself at a given moment."[3] The results of this attitude were inconsistencies stemming from the successful demands of nationalism or politics upon his idealism. These were concessions to human weakness. Had he demanded absolute adherence to his principles he would have been an ivory-tower idealist. He was an activist, pursuing a practical goal with the help of high moral values. He would have failed had he ignored the limits beyond which his people would not or could not have responded. From the standpoint of a leader with a mission to arouse his people to action, his willingness to tolerate inconsistencies was a virtue.

An additional difficulty in distentangling values from political goals or measuring the influence of values upon decisions is in the practice of using moral values as a political weapon, or, on the other hand, of denying them altogether for the sake of politics by admitting, as Gandhi occasionally did, that an undesirable means, such as a war, might produce a desirable end. At least his explanations of his noncombatant aid to the British in the Boer, Zulu, and First World Wars lend themselves to this interpretation. Nehru believed that as a nationalist politician Gandhi's "love of freedom for India and all other exploited nations and peoples overcame even his strong adherence to nonviolence."[4] It is not at all surprising that international affairs provided most of the occasions when Gandhi found himself obliged to tolerate a compromise with his own values. Among these values, nonviolence was the one most frequently interdicted. *Realpolitik* was the precipitating agent and nationalism the underlying cause creating the dilemmas.

The reason for the dilemmas, and Gandhi considered them such, was fairly obvious. Gandhi did not have the influence upon world affairs or other peoples that he possessed in his own country. Though his basic ideology encompassed mankind, and although he was well-informed about current events, the fate of his own country, the question of Indian independence, was his first and foremost concern. His action program was designed for India, though he considered it a precedent to be followed elsewhere. It did not suit all international relations equally well, at least not from the standpoint of a nationalist intent upon saving his country's political and territorial integrity under all circumstances occurring in a nation-state system. In such instances, Gandhi was willing to tolerate deviation from principle, though never to the point of betraying India's freedom.

This tolerance for deviation from ideology made possible great maneuverability for the policy maker without his having to contravene Gandhian principles. In comparing Gandhian values with some main features of Indian foreign policy, the point to remember is that Gandhi, the political practitioner, may be as "guilty" of deviations as any other foreign policy maker in India or elsewhere. On the other hand, a close correlation between Gandhi's ideology and an aspect of India's foreign policy may simply be due to the fact that Gandhi adjusted his values to political reality and requirements.

In examining Gandhian theory and Indian foreign policy, the greatest interest is concentrated on the use of violence in inter-state relations. In principle, Gandhi did not approve of violence in either inter-state or inter-personal relations. Nevertheless, he allowed numerous exceptions when they were based on considerations of high moral values. Gandhi, for instance, held that when the choice is between cowardice and violence, violence should be preferred. He taught that if one harbors violence, it is better to project it than to let it infect mind and spirit. Usually such statements were not made for the purpose of advocating violence but rather to avoid behavior or psychological unhappiness which Gandhi considered even more immoral or incompatible with truth than the use of violence.

Gandhi's own political actions in wars during his lifetime, and his evaluation of wars in which India was not directly involved, indicate quite clearly that he tolerated violent defense and that he thought it possible for violent national action to produce just ends. He knew that a modern state could not resist external aggression by nonviolent means; he taught that pacifists should not interfere with their government's violent defense against aggression; he approved of violence to win a nation's freedom and maintain its unity; and he admired the bravery of the Indian army in Kashmir. It is clear that Gandhi did not advocate absolute pacifism according to the rule that it is better to be killed than to kill. Whether he actively encouraged violent defense or whether he would personally have participated in violent action is less clear. It is also true, on the other hand, that he advised the Abyssinians, Chinese, Czechs, Poles and British to resist nonviolently after their countries were attacked.

Indian policy makers succeeding Gandhi, under great pressure to make practical decisions, could legitimately interpret his teachings as giving them great leeway between the use of violence and nonviolence in defense of Indian interests. The Indian government at any rate chose to reject nonviolence as a weapon in international affairs. Nehru was quite distinct about that choice. In answer to the Gandhian Acharya Kripalani, who asked whether the government was committed to nonviolence, the Indian prime minister replied, "The answer to that is no, the Government is not."[5] If it were committed to nonviolent means, he elaborated on this and other occasions, India would not have armed forces, possibly not even a police force.

Nehru, of course, understood the nuances and refinements of Gandhi's thought. He could have rested his case on some sophisticated interpretation and still have claimed adherence to Gandhian ideology. It is to his credit that he frankly admitted deviation or at least exploited Gandhi's tolerance toward those unable to live up to his ideals. Nehru explained that realism forced a statesman to defend the country in his charge by all available means; no other policy was possible. He added that nonviolence in practice required a greatness which Gandhi, but not the Indian people, possessed. By thus placing the Mahatma on a pedestal on which ordinary Indians could not join him, he permitted himself and his government to pursue a policy of armed defense and of violent action which, according to him, Gandhi would not have chosen. He admitted that this course of action troubled his mind. Though India was keeping armed forces, he recognized the futility of violence in international relations. But he chose the alternative of violence, nevertheless. He had far-reaching support in doing so.

At the same time, during the earlier years of his premiership, Nehru's government regularly engaged in moral appeals to the world. It criticized the behavior of other nations on moral grounds and justified its own policies on moral principles. Nehru's regime practiced this strategy with such insistence that other nations felt provoked. Nehru defended himself against accusations of a "holier than thou" attitude with the assurance that he was not "moralizing" anybody. Indians were deeply conscious of their own failings. He insisted that he was simply approaching international affairs with the outlook that Gandhi left to the world. He merely wanted to express the conviction, which he shared with Gandhi, that an improvement of international relations required actions based on high moral principles. The Indian government's refusal—when India did not consider herself the victim of aggression—to sponsor or sign condemnatory resolutions in the United Nations directed against law-breaking nations was a reflection of this approach. More specifically, it corresponded to the Gandhian conception of ahimsa. It also reflected Nehru's conviction that in a conflict the duty of the involved and third parties is not to engage in name-calling but to find a peaceful solution. Gandhi, similarly, advised pacifists whose country was at war not to wish success to their own country or to the enemy but to pray for the victory of right. That on many occasions the Indian government found it easier to practice what it preached in relation to the Communist nations than to the Westerners—dramatically highlighted in the Hungarian and Tibetan cases—is not really a denial of this approach but rather an indicator of the difficulty of taking it. Nevertheless, this differing behavior toward the Western and the Communist world, vigorously denied by the Indian government, created in many quarters abroad the impression of a double standard. Indian appeals to morality lost much of their convincing power. The suspicion arose, and not without some reason, that morality was misused for expedient purposes of the national interest.

Gandhi's advocacy of nonviolence by the Indian people against the British has likewise been subjected to some criticism of expediency. Gandhi made it fairly clear that India's posture was the "nonviolence of the weak," practiced because of a lack of weapons, rather than the nonviolence of the strong which he considered the highest form of his concept of nonviolence. It was practical and effective strategy against the colonialists within India which attracted attention and support from abroad. Because of this utility some confusion arose in the public's mind about measures advocated on moral and utilitarian grounds—a popular but quite unjustifiable dichotomy. Furthermore, when Gandhi stated that "in a society based on nonviolence, the smallest nation will feel as tall as the tallest," some criticism could be heard that another element of opportunism was introduced into appeals for greater morality in international relations. If these appeals had been heeded, physically weak India would have been the foremost beneficiary. Adherence to law and morality are the main weapons of weak or small states to obtain the legal and political equality they all crave. However, when Gandhi assumed a moral stance against Great Britain, the liberal world applauded him and could ignore any implication of self-interest. In the international climate prevailing at the time, morality was clearly on India's side and greater moral influence in world affairs would benefit all mankind.

When Nehru assumed the same posture as the leader of independent India, he could rightfully expect the same applause, providing he did so as a matter of principle under all circumstances. Otherwise, an inconsistent and selective use of morality would merely be a tool of expediency. Nehru did not maintain this consistency in his foreign policy in the judgment of some governments and observers. His failure to respond to India's own call for moral international behavior raised doubts about the sincerity of his moral convictions or his right to make moral criticisms of others. It provoked widespread opposition abroad to his moralizing. Whether Gandhi's behavior would have been subject to the same doubts is open to question in the light of his approving stance on India's actions in Kashmir.

There is little doubt that some of the methods that India used in her own neighborhood did not meet the standards by which she judged others. Examples are found in the crises in Hyderabad, Kashmir and Goa as well as in the pressure tactics applied to Nepal and the Nagas. The sharp criticism of Western militarism and security alliances was never applied to the military Sino-Soviet alliance of 1950. The reluctance to participate in international condemnation of law-breaking seemed to evaporate when India considered herself the victim of aggression, as, for instance, in regard to Pakistan or China in 1962. On the occasion of the Himalayan fighting India's usual insistence on nonaligned positions as the most useful contribution to the restoration of peace gave way to complaints that her fellow nonaligned states refused to side with her. And, as an American observer remarked, the sight of sari-clad girls goose-stepping during a military parade was rather shocking in a nation led to independence by Gandhi.[6]

This kind of behavior needs to be interpreted as a deviation from Gandhian principles only in the sense that it failed to reach Gandhi's ideals. In the actual execution of Indian foreign policy some qualities considered desirable had to be sacrificed to *Realpolitik* in favor of other qualities—a show of force among them —whose relations to Gandhian tenets were not, to say the least, obvious. Like all governments, India was guided by the preservation of national interests, whose interpretation and safeguarding were partially determined by the international system rather than Gandhian values and beliefs. In such situations there was consistency with nationalist elements of Gandhian ideology but inconsistency with other elements. But many were inconsistencies which Gandhi would presumably have tolerated. Considering the nature of the nation-state system, it appears inevitable that a difference must be allowed between overall general policy based upon high principles and daily tactics or even long-range strategy based upon practical considerations.

Nehru probably had this dilemma in mind when he told his Congress Parliamentary Party after the 1962 debacle in the Himalayas that abandonment of nonalignment as a policy would mean the loss of some vital part of the Gandhian heritage. Implied here was the claim that nonalignment in international politics was an attempt to shape Indian international behavior and influence in the image of Gandhian ideology, taking into account both its idealism and pragmatism. This was Nehru's understanding of the strategy.

How authentic is the linking of Gandhi to nonalignment? One of Gandhi's foremost goals and a *sine quo non* of his anticolonial policy was to give his people self-respect and an identity. Nonalignment aims at exactly those ends for India on the international scene. Attachment to any nation's foreign policy would have meant for the Indian elite a continuation of servility and a denial of self-expression. Nonalignment is, psychologically, the final confirmation of Indian independence. Nehru's terminology in justifying nonalignment often very distinctly reflected India's newly gained pride in national identity as well as her sense of responsibilty for determining her own fate. Nonalignment also opened the possibility for India to speak her mind freely and courageously. This, too, corresponded to a major effort of Gandhi to encourage his people and immunize them against intimidation. Fear was, to him, a great evil. Fear was immoral, because it was at the root of untruth. Fearlessness was the foundation of freedom; hence his stress upon its cultivation by his people. On innumerable occasions Nehru emphasized that his country's policy was not and never would be based on fear.

Fear was the root of violence, according to Gandhi. This view was transferred to the justification of nonalignment. Many times Nehru warned the world that mutual fear and suspicion were the causes of tensions and armaments. In tying this idea to the means and ends relationship he argued that preparing for war entails the danger of producing war. With Gandhi, he believed that no good end can be reached with evil means. An independent, nonaligned posture enabled India not only to remain aloof from international hostilities but positively to reduce them—or so the government hoped. Toward this end Gandhi's belief in the goodness of man was most helpful and was accepted in the operation of nonalignment. Gandhi harbored no ill will toward an opponent. The Mahatma was ready to cooperate with him, if he would abandon evil. He often assured his followers that the enemy was British imperialism not the British. At the same time he showed great tolerance for a variety of social systems and ideologies. The mediating role the Indian government could play as a result of nonalignment mirrored this attitude. Nehru specifically denied that ideologies even came into the picture in the hostilities between the United States and the Soviet Union. He traced their differences to clashing interests which could be settled by agreement. He shared with Gandhi a preference for synthesis of whatever was good regardless of source.

From this viewpoint came the preference of nonaligned statesmen for negotiations as the primary means for settling international problems. India showed a distinct dislike for the legal and compulsory means and methods of the United Nations. Indeed, she opposed both their application and further development, while she always favored (with the exceptions noted earlier) facilities for bringing contending parties to the conference table. She counselled as well as practiced moderation in the hope of producing agreement. Actually, there could be doubt that Gandhi would have fully approved of nonalignment when it meant not taking a position. He felt quite strongly that a nonviolent, neutral country should commit itself against a wrongdoing nation and help the victim by positive action, not merely by bringing both sides to the conference table. For this reason, for instance, he favored an Indian boycott against Japanese goods when Japan invaded China. Conceivably, Gandhi might have acted more decisively than the Indian government in the Korean war. Certainly, he would have done so in the Hungarian case.

There is a parallel between Gandhi, the nationalist, attracting the notice and possibly the sympathy of the world and nonalignment as an attention-getting device. Gandhi gave Indian nationalism an outer-directedness which no other nationalism possessed. Though he was aiming first and foremost at independence for his country, his concern embraced other suppressed countries and, in fact, suppressed men everywhere. His nationalism lacked the almost obsessive concern with sovereignty to be found in other Asian countries. He wanted a "voluntary interdependence of nations," a "federation of friendly, interdependent states." When Ralph Bunche once asked why it was assumed that in his actions Gandhi was concerned primarily with all humanity and only secondarily with Indians and India, Dr. Sarvepalli Radakrishnan replied that Gandhi took up the Indian cause not out of narrow patriotism, not only because he happened to belong to India, but because of his intense love for humanity and to demonstrate to humanity the possibility of changing its fate.[7] His principles expressed a world-wide yearning for an end to violence, a more liberal evaluation of freedom, the realization of political equality, and the creation of a brotherhood of man. These ideas were not new, but Gandhi stated them in terms making them more realistic. More important, Gandhi by his own actions demonstrated them to be feasible against the apparent opposition of the world's mightiest nation. And Gandhi was a mortal; indeed, he emphasized his equality with the common man. No god-like qualities were needed to make ideals become real. To enable ordinary men and women to put them into operation, Gandhi educated his people to lose fear, to gain self-respect, and, finally, to discipline their minds and actions. In so doing he made India a world-wide symbol of anti-colonialism.

As the major protagonist of nonalignment, Nehru took over this teacher role to some extent. Many of his speechees in Congress or at international conferences were, in fact, lessons. The large number of nonaligned states in South and Southeast Asia testifies to his success as a teacher. The attention and respect India commanded during the first decade of her independence could also be ascribed at least in part to her nonalignment posture. The gradual decline of India's prestige in the world and her waning influence were largely due to changes in the constellation of world conditions over which India had no control whatever. But a contributing factor was possibly also a change in the nature of Indian nationalism. With Gandhi it assumed a global mission; under his successors, this quality was lost.

Gandhi as an active political leader incorporated both idealistic and realistic components in his ideology. His continued influence in the sphere of international politics is the result of the severity with which he applied his values and beliefs to his own behavior; it is also the result of his demonstration by his practical success that ideals can, indeed, become reality. These achievements make it difficult for statesmen designing foreign policies to ignore consideration of moral values and ethical principles. Cynicism about normative constraints upon national behavior in a nationalistic world is easy enough. Yet it is undeniable that in the course of time, as larger portions of the public become involved in the making and execution of foreign policy, statesmen have increasingly felt the need to justify their decisions in moral terms. Gandhi was not the first man to push developments in this direction. By conducting his personal life in accordance with his ideology, he contributed more than any other man to this development. That it is slow to mature is due to the political culture of the international society.

NOTES

1. Werner Levi, *The Challenge of World Politics in South and Southeast Asia* (Englewood Cliffs, N. J.: Prentice-Hall, Inc., 1968), p. 21.
2. Paul F. Power, *Gandhi on World Affairs* (London: Allen and Unwin, 1961), p. 36. On the role of ideology in foreign policy, see Werner Levi, "Ideology, Interests, and Foreign Policy," *International Studies Quarterly* 14 (March 1970): 1-31.
3. Quoted in H. J. N. Horsburgh, *Non-Violence and Aggression* (London: Oxford University Press, 1968), p. 32.
4. Nehru, Jawaharlal, *India's Foreign Policy* (Delhi: Ministry of Information and Broadcasting, Government of India, 1961), p. 484.
5. *Ibid.*, p. 115.
6. Kenneth E. Boulding, "Why did Gandhi fail?" *Gandhi Marg* 8 (October 1964): 316.
7. *Gandhian Outlook and Techniques* (New Delhi: Ministry of Education, Government of India, 1953), pp. 111, 119.

COMPARATIVE PERSPECTIVES

7

RELIGIOUS REVOLUTIONARIES OF THE THIRD WORLD: GANDHI, GANDHIANS, AND *GUERRILLEROS*

Donald E. Smith

Most interpretations and assessments of Gandhi see him primarily as either an Indian figure or a universal figure. Some students of Gandhi are primarily concerned with his place in the history of Indian nationalism. Others have little interest in Indian history per se, and see Gandhi's significance in universal terms, in terms of what he called his "experiments with truth," the religious, philosophical, psychological and ethical dimensions of human existence. Needless to say, there are a number of students who are vitally concerned with both aspects.

I should like to suggest that there is an important intermediate context in which we must explore Gandhi, his ideas, and his political leadership. Gandhi was indeed an Indian figure and a universal figure, but he was also a man of the Third World. In speaking for the poor, the subjugated and the oppressed, he spoke for the masses of South and Southeast Asia, the Middle East, Africa and Latin America. As a man of the Third World, what did Gandhi say and do which is perceived as relevant today?

To raise the question of relevance implies some notion of the character of the contemporary Third World. Among the various common features of these areas, I would point especially to three which are fundamental: (1) poverty, (2) inequality and (3) rising discontent. These countries have predominantly agricultural economies and low productivity; per capita income is low. Their populations are divided into small upper classes, small middle classes, and vast majorities hovering precariously at the subsistence level. The rising discontent of the middle and lower sectors is not simply the consequence of poverty and inequality but is also related to factors such as the weakening of traditional social institutions, economic competition intensified by rapid population growth, the failure of government-directed programs of economic development, the propagation of radical egalitarian ideologies, etc.

Taken together, poverty, inequality and rising discontent represent a situation of growing revolutionary potential. In Asia and Africa, two decades and one decade, respectively, after independence, the legitimacy conferred on ruling groups by previous leadership in nationalist movements has largely evaporated. In Latin America, attitudes of profound cynicism toward all governments have long prevailed, and broad-based nationalist support of government is seemingly produced only by crises and conflicts with the United States.

The revolutionary potential of the Third World is growing. Nkrumah, Sukarno, and other charismatic leaders have failed in their efforts to perpetuate the mystique of a continuing nationalist revolution. Political independence has not brought about any massive restructuring of society or any major redistribution of power. Yet, this is the response which the situation of poverty, inequality and rising discontent seems to demand. Among most Latin American intellectuals, revolution is an unqualifiedly good word, and they are not referring to coups or palace revolts but to this radical restructuring of social power.

Revolutionary movements, or programs of planned revolutionary change, contain one or more of the following four elements.

1. *An ideology of radical social change.* Ideas alone, obviously, do not produce revolutionary change, but they

are usually an important component. A revolutionary ideology generally specifies the objectives and justifies the costs of change by relating the effort to transcendent principles of justice.

2. *The mobilization of the masses.* Many revolutionary theories emphasize the role of the masses. As the vast majority of the population, the masses (both urban and rural) must be involved to produce significant change. Present institutions function because the masses cooperate with them, and any radical change in their behavior is automatically revolutionary in nature.

3. *An explicit strategy of conflict.* As most revolutionaries see it, there can be little fundamental change in the power relationships of society without conflict. Whether the conflict is resolved by force or nonviolently, it must be recognized and planned for.

4. *Political power as a means of change.* Revolutionaries disagree radically on the role of political power; the majority view finds it inconceivable that any radical transformation of society as a whole can be brought about without utilizing the power of the state.

Revolutionary ideology, mass mobilization, strategy of conflict, and political power are listed simply as elements frequently found in movements of planned radical change. There are no normative assumptions concerning the elements essential to an authentic revolutionary program nor any assertions about the necessary and sufficient conditions of solid social transformation.

It is obvious that Marxism and its many variants represent the most influential body of theory concerning revolutionary change in the Third World today. In this paper, however, I should like to call attention to the thought of the religious revolutionaries. This subject has a special importance, I believe, because a fourth characteristic of the Third World (to be added to poverty, inequality, and rising discontent) is religiosity. The traditional cultures of this vast area are predominantly religious, despite the powerful secularizing forces which have both eroded and attacked them frontally over the past hundred years. Excluding parts of sub-Saharan Africa from this generalization, Third World cultures have been largely molded by the major religious systems—Hinduism, Buddhism, Islam and Catholicism —and religious values continue to be important in social behavior.

How does religion relate to revolutionary change? The most obvious relationship is that, by and large, traditional religions operate as a powerful set of values and structures which prevent change, legitimizing the powers that be and consecrating the conditions that be, including poverty and inequality. What most interests us here, however, is the fact that religious revoluionaries have in fact arisen in the Third World, that they have reinterpreted their respective sacred traditions, and that aspects of these sacred traditions have been found to be startlingly relevant to the four elements of a revolutionary program sketched out above. Thus, divine imperatives provide the ideological legitimation and impetus for revolutionary change. Sacred symbols become the vehicle by which the masses are drawn into the political process and mobilized for action. Religious principles are used to define the strategy of conflict, nonviolent or violent, and also the relationship of the movement to political power. Viewed thus, religious traditions would seem to offer unique resources not to be found in imported secular ideologies.

I shall now attempt to apply the preceding analysis to the religious revolutionaries who have appeared on the scene. The first category is that of Gandhiji himself, who must be counted among the few great revolutionary figures of history. In the second category, the Gandhians, I shall be chiefly concerned with Vinoba Bhave and the *sarvodaya* movement as it has evolved since Gandhi's death. In the third category I shall examine the *guerrilleros* (the Spanish word for guerrilla fighters), emphasizing the work of Father Camilo Torres, the young Catholic priest of Colombia whose revolutionary understanding of the Christian gospel led him to espouse armed conflict with government forces.

GANDHI:
SATYAGRAHA AND CONFLICT RESOLUTION

Gandhi's words and actions defy all efforts to pin simplistic labels on him—individualist, socialist, democrat, anarchist—all must be qualified so extensively that their usefulness is more than doubtful. There is certainly no desire here to use revolutionary as one more such label. It will be useful, however, to attempt to analyze Gandhi's thought and leadership in terms of the four aspects of planned revolutionary change mentioned above.

First, it is clear that Gandhi never articulated a well-defined ideology of radical social change. There were isolated ideas and emphases which could have provided the framework for such an ideology, but even the effort to formulate one was an enterprise quite foreign to Gandhi's basic premises. As he emphasized again and again, if the means are right, the end is bound to be right and hence should not be a matter of great concern. It was Gandhi's refusal to elaborate an over-all objective of social change, and not his emphasis on nonviolent means, which most baffled and exasperated his socialist colleagues in the Congress during the 1930's. Nehru, writes in his autobiography:

> What, after all, was he aiming at? In spite of the closest association with him for many years, I am not clear in my own mind about his objective. I doubt if he is clear himself. One step is enough for me, he says; and he does not try to peep into the future or to have a clearly conceived end before him. Look after the means, and the end will take care of itself, he is never tired of repeating. Be good in your personal individual lives, and all else will follow.[1]

Nehru's comment on this position was that:

> Vagueness in an objective seems to me deplorable. Action to be effective must be directed to clearly conceived ends. Life is

not all logic, and those ends will have to be varied from time to time to fit in with it, but some end must always be clearly envisaged.

Nine pages later Nehru returned to this theme, emphasizing that he was not concerned with the question of means—compulsion or conversion, violence or nonviolence.

But the necessity for the change must be recognized and clearly stated. If leaders and thinkers do not clearly envisage this and state it, how can they expect ever to convert anybody to their way of thinking, or develop the necessary ideology in the people?[2]

Despite Gandhiji's explicit statement that "the follower of Swadeshi never takes upon himself the vain task of trying to reform the world," there are elements of a revolutionary ideology in his thought which cannot be overlooked. Gandhi's strong assertion of reason and conscience as the sole criteria by which social institutions should be judged is profoundly revolutionary. He specifically asserted this claim against both custom and religious authority, and applied the principle in the most immediately relevant area of Indian social life, namely, the caste structure. Untouchability, the prohibitions on intercaste dining and marriage, and other aspects of caste were rejected along with the scriptural authority which sanctioned them. He wrote: "Assumption of superiority by any person over any other is a sin against God and man. Thus caste, insofar as it connotes distinctions in status, is an evil."[3] However, even here Gandhi's thought was not without its ambiguities, for he also produced an idealized interpretation of the original varna system. While this had degenerated over the centuries and was not seen by Gandhi as "an excrescence and a handicap on progress," the most logical implication would be the restoration of the ancient ideal rather than the complete abandonment of the caste idea. As has been clearly shown, Gandhi's thinking on the subject underwent a gradual evolution from a fairly orthodox position to one of egalitarianism in the social sphere.[4]

In the economic sphere, Gandhi took a considerably more conservative position regarding existing institutions. His statements envisaged a paternalistic socio-economic order; landlords were to function as trustees of their God-given wealth and were to take good care of their tenants. Needless to say, this is not compatible with the concept of a pluralist society in which power is widely distributed. Gandhi rejected industrial society and opposed technological modernization. His ideal was the largely self-sufficient village community, and he evidenced no interest at all in economic development for its own sake. He envisaged relatively greater economic equality but at a low level of material wealth. Gandhi saw materialism as a greater threat to society than either poverty or inequality. The spiritual values which were primary for him were best realized by self-restraint, even asceticism, and material prosperity was more likely to corrupt than to liberate man.

Gandhi developed, therefore, no clear ideology of radical social change. His emphasis on judging the validity of institutions by reason and conscience was a powerful intellectual tool, but this was significantly used only in dealing with the problems of caste. It must be remembered, however, that the struggle for political independence was the basic context in which Gandhi's leadership developed. The objective of *swaraj* was perfectly clear, and for this reason Nehru and other critics willingly followed Gandhi, however much they regretted his conservatism or imprecision regarding the desired shape of society.

Secondly, Gandhi's revolutionary leadership was brilliantly demonstrated in the mobilization of the masses. And here we see most clearly the significance of the religious aspect of his political leadership. The masses, and many of Gandhi's close associates, found in him a Mahatma, one who in some way incarnated and communicated the divine. Gandhi spoke of political struggle in religious terms; the struggle against the British was to achieve Rama Raj, the victory of Rama (good) over Ravana (evil). In his daily prayer meetings, in his frequent references to the Gita, in his vow of *brahmacharya,* and in the religious premises and overtones of satyagraha (discussed below), Gandhi spoke directly to the masses steeped in the language and symbols of traditional Hindu religion.

Our point here should not obscure the significance of the non-Hindu aspects of Gandhi's mobilization of the masses. Gandhi also used powerful nonreligious symbols, such as khadi. It was the Indian National Congress with its secular orientation which provided most of the organizational support for his mass political movement. And, very important, it was Gandhi's vigorous identification of Islamic religious symbols (the caliphate, in particular) with the non-cooperation movement which made possible the united Hindu-Muslim opposition to British rule during that brief period. However, it could be argued that Gandhi's recognition of the validity of other religions (institutionalized in his prayer meetings through readings from the Koran and New Testament as well as the Gita) was in itself a peculiarly Hindu form of universalism.

Thirdly, Gandhi's revolutionary strategy of conflict was worked out in the theory and practice of satyagraha. Stripped of all rhetoric, satyagraha was a technique for creating a confrontation with an adversary (individual or institution) whose acts or relationships with others were regarded as unjust; in this confrontation the satyagrahi applied nonviolent moral pressure on the adversary, refusing to retaliate if attacked violently. Satyagraha organized on a mass scale and directed against a foreign imperialist government became a technique of compelling dramatic power. Far from side-stepping conflict, satyagraha deliberately precipitated it, but insisted on the nonviolent approach to its resolution, however violent the response of the adversary might be.

The religious significance of satyagraha was absolutely fundamental in Gandhi's thought. Satyagraha—holding on to Truth, or Truth-force—must be linked to Gandhi's statements that Truth "is the only correct and fully significant name for God," and that ahimsa (nonviolence) and self-suffering are the means to Truth. Gandhi's expositions of satyagraha struck deeply responsive chords in the more traditional Hindu mind and heart, although many of his colleagues in the Congress accepted the new action technique on highly pragmatic grounds. As one writer noted: "Congress, however, lacked his faith. He carried the vote [in 1920] not because of any deep-seated Ahimsa but because constitutionalism and terrorism were both bankrupt."[5]

Finally, we must inquire into Gandhi's attitude toward political power in relationship to planned revolutionary change. To begin with, it is clear that *swaraj*, the capture of political power from the British, was the whole point of his movement. But what to do with political power once it was achieved? Here Gandhi's statements are not too explicit, and his assassination came so soon after independence that we can only speculate as to his probable reaction to later developments. Gandhi certainly held up the ideal of the small community based on voluntary coopera- tion and felt that entire national societies could be organized in this nonviolent way with a minimum of state control. He ob- served in 1935: "I look upon an increase in the power of the state with the greatest fear, because, while apparently doing good by minimizing exploitation, it does the greatest harm to mankind by destroying individuality, which lies at the root of all progress."[6] Whatever revolutionary social change Gandhi envisaged for India (and as we have seen, this was never spelled out in a coherent ideology), political power was not to be the primary means for bringing it about.

GANDHIANS: VINOBA BHAVE AND *BHOODAN*

The *sarvodaya* movement under Vinoba Bhave's leader- ship represents in some respects a continuation but in others a distinct departure from Gandhi's techniques and style of revolu- tionary action. In fact, it would be true to say that Vinoba has developed and enlarged the neglected ideological aspect of Gandhi's legacy, has paid much less attention to mass mobilization, has articulated no strategy of conflict, and has consistently spurned political power even when proffered.

Vinoba's revolutionary ideology has been eloquently and forcefully set forth. He wrote:

> Our work consists in changing the present social order from the very root. This is the secret of this Bhoodan campaign. That is why when people ask me whether this can be done by legislation alone, I reply in the negative. This is not a one-sided movement. When it succeeds the state will change, the government will change and the life-structure will change.[7]

While Gandhi was reluctant to state his objectives in terms of changing socio-economic structures, Vinoba has manifested no such inhibitions. In a remarkable address, Vinoba compared Communism and *sarvodaya:* He asserted that the former was generated by compassion and associated himself not only with its ultimate goal (the classless, stateless society) but with the revolutionary changes which are necessary steps, but disagreeing fundamentally with the Communists' espousal of violent means.

> What do we find today? We see that some people who are always talking of peace in actual effect believe in *status quo*. They are afraid of a change in human society. As against this, people who want a social revolution do not want to confine themselves within the four walls of *Ahimsa*. . . . But what are we? We are revolutionaries but we work peacefully.[8]

Vinoba's revolutionary message to the villagers is couched in traditional Hindu metaphors and mythological references.

> The most essential requisite of Samyayogi social structure is that all land, all property, and all wealth should belong to society. Only Vishnu can be the lord of Lakshmi, a seat which you have usurped. . . . Lakshmi is mother, and we are her

children. On the contrary, today we aggrandise ourselves as her Lord. I feel this is injustice, and a denial of religion.[9]

By this masterful reinterpretation of a traditional motif, the goddess of wealth is seen as the victim of greedy landlords, while her proper role is that of mother-provider to all her children equally.

There has been little mass mobilization of an organized nature in the *bhoodan* movement. Vinoba's primary technique has simply been to walk from village to village, holding meetings attended by virtually everyone living in a given vicinity, and appealing publicly to the landlords present to give one-sixth or more of their land for distribution to the landless peasants. Unlike Gandhi's satyagraha campaigns, there is no strategy of conflict. There is simply a moral appeal issued to the landlords, and whatever response is made, whether positive or negative, is accepted. Vinoba has in fact insisted that any land given because of a threat or under other compulsion be given back to the owner.

Vinoba's rejection of political power as the key to revolutionary change is rooted in the conviction that social values are more basic than structures. Structural changes brought about by coercive legislation will be frustrated because the same old social values continue to motivate behavior. Specifically, Vinoba points to the widely acknowledged limitations of governmental land-reform programs carried out since independence. Theoretical considerations aside, land-reform legislation and supporting development programs have failed to produce the large-scale agrarian revolution which was the professed objective.[10]

At the same time, Vinoba's program has run into major problems. Vinoba's distrust of bureaucratic organization has left him without adequate tools to deal with the over one hundred thousand entire villages which have been gifted to his movement. While the results thus far achieved would have been thought impossible in 1951, and there is no desire to minimize the significance of what has taken place, few Indian observers outside the movement regard it as the revolutionary breakthrough to far-reaching social change which was once hoped.

GUERRILLEROS: CAMILO TORRES
AND THE CATHOLIC REVOLUTIONARIES

Throughout Latin America, the name of Camilo Torres is probably as well known as those of Gandhi and Vinoba in India. Born in Bogota, Colombia, in 1929, to an influential upper-class family, Camilo studied for the Catholic priesthood in a Dominican seminary.[11] After his ordination he went to Brussels to begin graduate work in sociology at the University of Louvain, received the M.A. degree and began work on the doctorate. He returned to Colombia to begin the research for his dissertation, became chaplain at the National University and also a member of the Department of Sociology.

He published a number of articles on his empirical sociological research, but from 1961 on devoted himself increasingly to the development of a social theory which could deal with the realities of Colombian society. In this period he found aspects of Marxian theory to be highly relevant, and by mid-1965 was preparing himself for direct political action. Camilo sought to bring together all Colombian revolutionary elements, Catholic, Marxist, and others, in a United Front. His open denunciations of the dominant oligarchy, which controlled Colombian society through both church and state, brought him into conflict with the conservative ecclesiastical hierarchy. In 1965, after more than ten years in the priesthood, he petitioned the Cardinal for reduction to the lay state, which was granted. Torres later wrote:

> I have left the duties and the privileges of the clergy, but I have not stopped being a priest. I believe that I have given myself to the revolution out of love of my neighbor. I have stopped saying Mass in order to realize that love of neighbor in the temporal, economic and social sphere. When I have accomplished the revolution, I will again offer Mass, if God permits.[12]

Camilo's efforts to unite the various leftist groups in the country failed, and finally, in late 1965, he went to the mountains of eastern Colombia to join the guerrilla group which called itself the Army of National Liberation. On February 15, 1966, he was killed in a clash with government forces. Camilo Torres' revolutionary message, however, has had an enormous impact throughout Latin America, from Mexico to Chile.

Torres' ideology of radical social change, while supported by Marxist elements, was authentically grounded in Christian principles which were stated in the simplest of terms. He wrote:

> The main principle in Catholicism is love of neighbor. "He who loves his neighbor fulfills the law." (St. Paul, Romans 13:8). In order to be true this love must seek to be effectual. If benevolences, alms, the few free schools, the few housing projects, what has been called "charity," do not succeed in giving food to the majority of the hungry, nor clothing to the majority of the naked, nor instruction to the majority of the uneducated, we have to seek effective measures for the welfare of the majority. Privileged minorities who have power are not going to seek those measures, because generally those effective measures compel the minorities to sacrifice their privileges. . . . It is necessary, then, to take power away from the privileged minorities and to give it to the poor majority. This, if it is done rapidly, is the essence of a revolution.[13]

Torres argued that "the Revolution is not only permitted but obligatory for Christians who see in it the only effective and full way to achieve love for all."

The mobilization of the masses had high priority in Camilo's revolutionary program. The means he attempted to utilize, however, were indirect. He tried to unite the numerous organized groups in Colombian society—students, trade unions, leftist political parties, peasant groups, etc.—behind his United Front platform. This detailed platform called for the creation of a socialist society and for opposition to United States imperialism. Camilo sought to bring together the revolutionary, or potentially revolutionary, elements through mass propaganda, innumerable public meetings, the periodical *Frente Unido*, and other means. One of the major reasons for the failure of the effort was the inability of the leftist parties to transcend personal and ideological differences in order to work for revolutionary unity.

Camilo's strategy of conflict underwent changes as his movement progressed. He rejected the United Front's participation in national elections as a political party; this would have tended to divide, not unify, the opposition, and furthermore, he regarded fair elections as impossible since the oligarchy controlled the electoral machinery. After the failure of the United Front he opted for violent struggle. In justifying the resort to arms he cited the long Catholic tradition which sanctioned just wars and the legitimacy of insurrections against tyrants.

For Torres, it is clear, the seizure of political power by "the People" was the key to revolutionary change. He seems not to have been troubled at all by the thought that political power also might have its limitations in the transformation of societies.

Camilo Torres is dead, but the revolutionary impulses to which he gave expression are still being felt within Latin American Catholicism. Even within the Catholic hierarchy voices are being raised which, while regretting Camilo's mistakes, still find his call for revolutionary change the most authentic word which the Church has for Latin America and the Third World. Dom Helder Camara, Archbishop of Recife, Brazil, recently declared that the underdeveloped world desperately needs a "structural revolution." While asserting that his personal vocation was to peace and nonviolent methods, he added:

> I respect those who in conscience feel obligated to opt for violence, not the too easy violence of the drawing-room guerrilla fighters, but those who have proved their sincerity by the sacrifice of their lives. It seems to me that the memory of Camilo Torres and Che Guevara merit as much respect as that of the pastor Martin Luther King.[14]

CONCLUSIONS: GANDHI, VINOBA, TORRES

In examining these three religious revolutionaries we have sought to call attention to a significant phenomenon of the Third World—radically reformulated religion providing the vital impulse for radical social change. It cannot be claimed that any of the three leaders has been strikingly successful in producing the social revolution envisioned. (I am thinking here of internal societal change, not anti-imperialist struggles such as that waged by Gandhi.) But the fact is that the world has seen very few examples of truly revolutionary change for all of the revolutionary rhetoric which has been disseminated from so many quarters. The totalitarian Russian and Chinese revolutions are still our best examples if we are thinking in terms of planned revolutionary change. Yet, it would appear that since 1945 the continuing technological revolution in Western society has produced internal societal changes which are hardly less significant although unplanned.

In making these observations our point is that Gandhi, Vinoba, and Torres cannot be evaluated as revolutionaries, not even by the pragmatic criterion of results achieved. It will be useful, however, to summarize the emphases in their revolutionary programs discussed above, and I shall then offer some highly tentative, highly subjective comments of my own without pretending that they are anything more than this. The following chart summarizes our analysis.

ELEMENTS OF A REVOLUTIONARY PROGRAM

	GANDHI	VINOBA	TORRES
Ideology Articulation		X	X
Mass Mobilization	X		X
Strategy of Conflict	X		X
Political Power	(X)*		X

* *swaraj* as objective

Gandhi's greatness as a revolutionary leader, it is clear, lay in his recognition of the latent power of the Indian masses, in his skill in infusing them with courage and militancy, and in developing a technique for precipitating conflict and then resolving it nonviolently. While the most dramatic and widespread uses of satyagraha came in the struggle against the British Raj, Gandhi also utilized it in his campaign against untouchability (the Vykom Temple Road satyagraha, for example) and in labor disputes (the Ahmedabad Labor satyagraha). Nevertheless, with independence satyagraha lost most of its steam and in the years following was often used irresponsibly. Gandhi left no revolutionary ideology which might guide and inspire later satyagrahis. The formulation of such an ideology was Vinoba's great contribution, and by applying this directly to the problem of land, he placed the *sarvodaya* movement at the very center of a major arena of change. But *Bhoodan,* despite its moral grandeur, had other weaknesses. Unlike satyagraha, it sidestepped the fundamental fact of conflicting interests in society and sought to produce change without conflict. Coercion, represented by political power, was given a very minor role in the overall scheme of things. Camilo Torres' revolutionary program included all four elements, but in the short-run at least he produced less objective change than either Gandhi or Vinoba. Torres recognized Marxist humanism as containing important, valid elements which made cooperation in the revolutionary process possible. For many to whom nonviolence is not an absolute ethical principle, Camilo's abrupt decision to become a *guerrillero* was tactically wrong. A charismatic figure of great appeal to the masses, Camilo could probably have done far more to mobilize the Colombian people to demand major socio-economic change. On the other hand, Father Camilo Torres, the martyr, has probably had greater influence than any other Catholic symbol of change.

Gandhi, then, was a man of the Third World. The principles which he enunciated and incarnated are part of the legacy of all men, but are most clearly relevant to those whose collective existence is characterized by poverty, inequality, and rising discontent. We have suggested that Gandhian principles, deeply rooted in religious perceptions of reality, are in fact competing with other revolutionary ideas, some of which are rooted in different religious perceptions. Gandhian ideas of revolutionary social change, it is clear, compete at a disadvantage. The general erosion of absolutes in the thinking and behavior of modern man, and the very urgency of the demand for radical change, make increasingly unlikely the acceptance of Gandhi's central point that means are more important than ends. Gandhi, however, will not be forgotten; his vision will continue to disturb men even if it does not guide their behavior.

NOTES

1. Jawaharlal Nehru, *Toward Freedom* (Boston: Beacon Press, 1961), pp. 313-14.
2. *Ibid.,* p. 323.
3. Quoted in Joan V. Bondurant, *Conquest of Violence* (Princeton: Princeton University Press, 1958), pp. 168-69.
4. See Dennis Dalton, "The Gandhian View of Caste, and Caste after Gandhi," in *India and Ceylon: Unity and Diversity,* ed. Philip Mason (New York: Oxford University Press, 1967), pp. 159-81.
5. Geoffrey Ashe, *Gandhi* (New York: Stein and Day, 1968), p. 206.
6. Quoted in Bondurant, *Conquest of Violence,* p. 175.
7. Acharya Vinoba Bhave, *The Principles and Philosophy of the Bhoodan Yagna* (Tanjore: Sarvodaya Prachuralaya, 1955), p. 1.
8. Wm. T. de Bary, ed., *Sources of Indian Tradition* (New York: Columbia University Press, 1964), 2:377.
9. Bhave, *The Principles . . . of the Bhoodan Yagna,* p. 2.

10. Hallam Tennyson, *India's Walking Saint* (New York: Doubleday & Co., 1955), pp. 82-83.
11. The first biography to appear in English is German Guzman, *Camilo Torres* (New York: Sheed and Ward, 1969).
12. *Ibid.*, p. 292.
13. "Mensaje a los cristianos," in *Camilo Torres, por el Padre Camilo Torres Restrepo* (1956-1966) (Cuernavaca, Mexico: Centro Intercultural de Documentacion, 1966), p. 325. For an English translation of this collection, see Camilo Torres, *Revolutionary Writings* (New York: Herder and Herder, 1969).
14. Dom Helder Camara, "La Violencia: Opcion Unica?" *Informaciones catolicas internacionales,* May 2, 1968, p. 7. For an English translation of the archbishop's writings, see Helder Camara, *The Church and Colonialism: The Betrayal of the Third World* (Denville, N. J.: Dimension Books, 1969).

8

GANDHIAN VALUES AND THE
AMERICAN CIVIL RIGHTS MOVEMENT

William Stuart Nelson

The principle that every human being is entitled to certain rights of being and development is an idea which has been perennially discussed by many philosophers throughout man's career on earth. It has been upheld and defended in whole or in part, renounced and ridiculed, and subjected to endless debate. The ideal has been advanced by social and political philosophers and by activists and denounced as a cruel hoax by conservatives and self-styled realists. Because Mahatma Gandhi has been an ardent advocate of this principle, his expression of the ideal deserves to be reexamined in some detail.

For Americans the principle existed before the Revolution and the founding of our nation. Early proponents were Roger Williams and Thomas Paine. Borrowing from John Locke and his contemporaries, Thomas Jefferson enunciated it as a self-evident truth—"that all men are created equal, that they are endowed by their Creator with certain unalienable rights. . . ." Although a slaveholder, Jefferson never departed from this principle nor did he consider his role as encroacher upon other men's freedom as anything more than an expedient to be corrected as soon as circumstances permitted. He and his associates in idealism have encouraged millions of Americans to believe that a sound state requires the expression of this principle above all others, regardless of the time it takes to bring about its fulfillment. In t¹ e mid-nineteenth century a supporter of this view was the anti-materialist Henry David Thoreau whose declarations on the subject of the right and the necessity of civil disobedience deeply impressed Gandhi.

The most fundamental ideals of life transcend the confines of nation and continent and are subject only to the boundaries of human experience. It is reasonable, therefore, to expect the Gandhian principle of human rights to be discussed and explored profitably in the United States. A most significant test of the principle is obviously possible in its application to American Negroes who for generations have been considered by some as comparable to Indian "untouchables." Of urgent relevance to this fact is the civil rights movement.

The ethic of nonviolence is the highest manifestation of belief in human equality and human rights. It is important to bear in mind that this ethic has been upheld by a considerable number of Americans, who have lived and died by it, from the seventeenth century onward. In effect, America was the host and teacher of the ethic. No less a pacifist than Leo Tolstoy, in "A Message to the American People," credited Garrison, Parker, Emerson, Ballou and Thoreau for influencing him. In his documentary history of nonviolence in America, Staughton Lynd points out that from William Penn and John Woolman to Jane Addams and Martin Luther King, Jr., America has more often been a teacher than a student of the nonviolent idea.[1] In the course of its application in America, the concept has changed. Prior to the Revolution small Christian sects interpreted it as literal obedience to the teaching of Jesus concerning non-resistance to evil. This led its devotees to seek reconciliation with the Indians, to appeal for the abolition of slavery and, at times, to break the law rather than disobey their consciences. Since the Revolution, secular studies have joined Christian sources to provide reasons for the prescription of nonviolence. Thus, William James placed emphasis on the psychological roots of nonviolence. In an older tradition, Martin Luther King, Jr. returned to the concept of nonviolence as religious with the understanding that he urged that the ethic was a social as well as personal guide to redemption.

Even though the United States has been in part a school for nonviolence, it is, nevertheless, indebted to recent exemplars of the ethic, especially to Gandhi. A major transmission belt was contact between Gandhi and Christian Negro leaders. The first known contact between Gandhi and American Negro leaders was Gandhi's reception of Dr. Howard Thurman, then professor at Howard University, and the Reverend Edward Carrol, and their wives, on February 28, 1936. Their discussion turned in part on the racial question in the United States. To a query put by the visitors, Gandhi proclaimed nonviolence as the greatest and most active force in the world. He stressed activism. "One cannot," he told his guests, "be passively nonviolent."[2] Gandhi had still a broader message. After listening to Dr. Thurman explain that American Negroes had a Christian tradition conducive to Gandhi's philosophy and that they were ready to practice it, Gandhi said: "Well, if it comes true, it may be through the Negroes that the unadulterated message of nonviolence will be delivered to the world."[3]

The next year, Dr. Channing Tobias, then a National Secretary of the Young Men's Christian Association, and Dr. Benjamin Mays, then Dean of the School of Religion of Howard University, met with Gandhi in Sevagram. Dr. Mays expressed his own faith in nonviolence but spoke with concern of the difficulty of disciplining the mass mind on the point of love.[4] How does one meet the problem, he asked, when the mass of the people break away from this ideal? In answer Gandhi advised him to adopt a long-run program of teaching and practice to include the symbols of nonviolence which must be internalized to become effective. Gandhi also dealt with the question of a minority facing an oppressive majority, holding that numbers are not vital to the ethic of nonviolence which is valid apart from such tactical issues.

Perhaps the most significant of my own meetings with Gandhi was in August 1947. India had just won its independence, and there were painful discussions about the results of partition. There was more than discussion in Calcutta where Hindu-Muslim tensions had broken into large-scale fighting and killing. Responding to the tragedy, Gandhi went to Calcutta to mediate and to attempt to bring peace. I was living in Calcutta at the time and had the opportunity to meet with him occasionally during this traumatic period. At one meeting, my last before returning to America, I asked why it was that Indians who had more or less successfully gained independence through peaceful devices were now unable to check the tide of civil war through the same means. Gandhi replied that my question was a searching one which he must answer. He confessed that it had become clear to him that what he had mistaken for satyagraha was not true satyagraha, but passive resistance—a weapon of the weak. Against the spirit of ahimsa, he explained, Indians had harbored ill will and anger towards their erstwhile rulers while pretending to resist them nonviolently. Their resistance had been informed by himsa, error or violence, instead of respect for the essential man in the British opponent.

Gandhi observed that with the British exit from India the apparent nonviolence disintegrated. As a result Indians flew at each other's throats, when the question of the distribution of power arose. It would be a great day, he said, if India could discover a way of sublimating the force of violence which had taken a communal turn and turning it into constructive, peaceful ways. He then declared his faith that India would rise above communalism and prove to the world that India and Pakistan were a blessing, not a menace, to mankind. The immediate duty of India, he said, was to perfect the instrument of nonviolence for dissolving internal conflicts.

As I recall this conversation with Gandhi I have two impressions: Gandhi's profound dedication to truth and his compassion for the masses. As to the Hindu-Muslim carnage, he could have launched into bitter criticism of the people who had acted toward the British as if they believed wholeheartedly in non-violence, only to betray themselves in Calcutta in retaliation against fellow Indians of another religious persuasion. But from Gandhi there came no bitter words towards these unfortunates. They, too, were God's sons; Gandhi's duty was to reconcile and not to blame them. For highest among Gandhi's spiritual qualities was his sense of compassion. If he could dampen the raging fires of bitterness in the Indian community and repeatedly express concern for American Negroes, it was because he had abundant compassion. Nowhere did his compassion show more deeply than in his dedication to the cause of the "untouchables."

Gandhi fought untouchability with his life. When in 1932 a new constitution for India was being written by the British in consultation with Indians, provision was made for a separate electorate by which the depressed classes could select their own representatives to the provincial legislatures. This device offended the then imprisoned Gandhi so deeply that he embarked upon a "fast to the death" to prevent its adoption. He argued that the special treatment would doom the "untouchables" to a permanent separation from their fellow-citizens. It would place a stamp of permanence upon a despised institution which he was determined to destroy. The plan for the separate electorate was compromised. Gandhi broke his fast with assurance to his *Harijan* friends that they might hold his life as hostage for the fulfillment of his goal of complete emancipation.

On January 26, 1950, when the Constitution of India came into force, Article 17 of the Constitution abolished untouchability and prohibited its practice in any form. When the Constituent Assembly approved the Article, its members arose and shouted: "Gandhiji ki jai." Here was one fruit of Gandhi's long and unremitting struggle against a great wrong. Here was another Emancipation Proclamation.

Let me now turn to Gandhi's relevance for the American scene. Among American disciples of Gandhi was James Farmer, for some years the director of the Congress of Racial Equality

(CORE). Mr. Farmer served also as program director of the National Association for the Advancement of Colored People (NAACP). Beginning in 1956, he dedicated himself to vital leadership in the American civil rights movement. He became an Assistant Secretary of the Department of Health, Education and Welfare in the Nixon Administration. He died in 1971.

In his book, *Freedom, When?,* Mr. Farmer told the story of the influence of Gandhi upon him and, through him, upon the civil rights movement in America.[5] Mr. Farmer described the motivation of his nonviolent discipleship. As always there was the Negro, a full fledged soldier on the battlefields of France, but at home still the son of Ham, a servant unto his brethren. Mr. Farmer became an ardent contestant in the struggle against violence, especially of the kind used against his fellow Negroes. He was involved in numerous sit-ins, freedom rides, and other actions to eliminate racial segregation without using unethical means.

According to James Farmer, the attempt to apply Gandhi's methods to the American race problem was extremely audacious. He suggested that the Indian scene had certain advantages not found in the American culture, among them Hinduism's symbolic interpretation of conflict and its tradition of self-abnegation so important to disciplined protest. Most important was the fact that in Gandhi the Indian movement had been blessed by an unparalleled leader who combined strategic brilliance and the charisma of a saint. Nonetheless, Farmer saw links to facilitate Gandhian resistance in the United States. One bond was the Gandhi-Thoreau nexus. Another stemmed from the current of activism in American social history. He believed that the tendency of Americans to act, as Gandhi did, rather than to withdraw, would help to import Gandhism and to offset passive elements in the American peace movement. Moreover, Farmer saw in Gandhi's assumptions about the power of love and righteousness a resemblance to the principles taught by Jesus in the Sermon on the Mount which had found their way into the heart of the Biblical Christianity of Negroes.

Farmer and his young associates in CORE believed that the justice of their demands would convert the segregationists. Good will and nonviolence would unlock their hearts. The idealists had not yet experienced police dogs and cattle prods. Another side of their dream was to emulate Gandhi's village programs by encouraging rural Negroes to produce hand-made crafts in a program of economic and psychological self-help. Farmer and his colleagues were ready to remake the country before they knew all of its realities. But they did go forward. After frustrating and harassing experiences in the struggle against racial segregation, they learned of the complexities and disappointments of any reform movement.

The years 1956-1968 marked an epoch in American history. These were the years when Martin Luther King, Jr. and James Farmer and thousands of other men and women and children, in the spirit of Mohandas K. Gandhi, marched, were beaten, sent to prison and even died in a courageous search for freedom. Special mention must be made of King's relation to Gandhi.

Martin Luther King, Jr., apostle of the nonviolent way of life and martyr to its cause, strode briefly but brilliantly across our times. Of the many formative influences in his life, there were two of central significance. The first was an address in 1950 by Dr. Mordecai Johnson, President of Howard University, at the Fellowship House of Philadelphia. A senior at Crozer Theological Seminary in nearby Chester, King went to hear the famous educator. Dr. Johnson had recently returned from India where the warm embers of his deep admiration for Gandhi had been blown into a flame. Gandhi was the subject of the address. Among Gandhi's qualities which Dr. Johnson stressed was his demonstration of the redemptive power of love as an instrument of nonviolent social reform. Prepared by other ideas and experiences, King welcomed the message and immediately pursued Gandhi's own writings about ahimsa and satyagraha. Later, he testified that he had found in Dr. Johnson's discussion of Gandhi and love the possible answer to the question as to how one can struggle for self-fulfillment and the common welfare without violence or surrender.[6] The answer which Gandhi gave may well have influenced the responses which Dr. King made to the several moral issues that confronted him from the Montgomery bus boycott in 1955-56 onward.

The second major influence in King's life was the bombing of his home in Montgomery on January 30, 1956. An angry crowd of friends gathered, and Dr. King heard a Negro challenge a policeman, who was attempting to push him aside, to a pistol duel. Dr. King's instant response was to calm the man's anger and to persuade the crowd that retaliation would be wrong. Violence, he told them, must be met with nonviolence. These few words told a great story. The Gandhian ideal had been written upon Dr. King's heart and into his life. It deepened as time went on and the trials mounted.

Dr. King faced many problems in his brief but fateful career. Throughout he kept the profoundly compassionate quality of his leadership that attracted the attention and respect of so many in the United States and abroad. The quality derived in part from his Christian family and ministerial training and to a degree from certain Gandhian values. He saw a particular confluence of three currents—the nonviolent resistance of the early Christians, the religious tradition of the Negro, and the ethical struggle of Mahatma Gandhi and his followers against the British Empire. One thing further we should remember as we comment on Dr. King's phenomenal career is that it was at times attended by serious problems. His struggle with them casts even clearer light upon his extraordinary character and abilities. He was fortunate in his many loyal followers who comprised not only the deeply loyal and able, but also the timid, the inept, the radical, and the bitter. Facing his problems in these contexts, Dr. King revealed extraordinary insight and fortitude. It is these gifts which help explain why he received the Nobel Peace Prize in 1964.

The year before, Howard University in Washington sponsored a conference on nonviolence which evoked a surprisingly large and favorable response from university personnel, students, townspeople, and visitors from afar. At the closing session there was one dissident note, spoken by Stokely Carmichael, then a senior in the College of Liberal Arts of the University. It provoked no special response. But it is now remembered as an omen of what was to come—Black Power—a term projected by Carmichael the next year in Greenwood, Mississippi. The term was born in a state where in three years more than forty Negroes and whites had either been lynched or otherwise murdered and no man brought to justice for the crimes. How does the Gandhian message relate to this development in American Negro history?

First of all, one should be mindful that, like Gandhian struggle, Black Power has many meanings. James Farmer had developed a version that combines the idealism of pacifists and the aggressiveness of those he called the New Jacobins. These Negroes became disillusioned with America's rhetoric of equality and saw in direct action a useful weapon in which nonviolence was only a tactic. In his new phase, Farmer denied that the Negro Revolution, which followed the early civil rights movement, is a hate movement, although he conceded that love is no longer the watchword and some haters can be found. He explained: "We have changed but only because we have learned from experience of our twenty years that the world is more complex than we imagined and the techniques and *motives* necessary to change it more varied and larger in scope than we had ever dreamed."[7] Moreover, Farmer stressed that the Negro rights movement has become a mass movement with an arsenal of techniques. Impatience has emerged as a virtue. The vision of reconciliation has not been discarded. Yet love does seem a luxury, although for Farmer nonviolence remained the best means.

What of Black Power and Dr. King? To him, the entry of the Black Power slogan into his movement was unexpected and unwelcome. No persuasion by Dr. King could prevent the contagion of the Black Power fever, especially with its encouragement by the press. He had to face what he conceived to be a nihilistic philosophy born of the Negro's inability to win otherwise in the struggle for his rights. Personal trauma followed the negative shouts by Black Power advocates which later greeted his speeches. He was not deterred, however, in his effort to lay bare the weaknesses of the slogan and to preach a better way. To him, it was a cry of despair and disappointment.

Black Power was not altogether repugnant to him. He saw it as a Negro effort to mobilize political and economic strength to achieve legitimate goals. He appreciated its psychological effort to wipe from the Negro's memory the insinuation that he is a nobody, biologically depraved and worthless, and to secure a kind of independence from whites, a second emancipation. But all these, he held, were the objectives of the civil rights movement before Black Power was born.

King especially objected to Black Power's implication of separatism which he believed to be deadly. In separation, he argued, there is no possibility of effective political power, no insurance against social injustice, no gain in economic power. On the contrary, the ability to enter into alliances has been a mark both of the Negro's strength and his weakness. "[T]here is," writes Dr. King, "no separate black path to power and fulfillment that does not intersect white paths. . . . We are bound together in a single garment of destiny."[8]

But above all it was the call for retaliatory violence which Dr. King regarded as the most destructive aspect of Black Power. In sadness, he admitted the use of the Black Power slogan principally by those who had lost faith in the method of nonviolence. Here is a parallel with Gandhi amidst the havoc of Calcutta. He further pointed to the danger of organizing a movement around "self-defense," since this concept often becomes an invitation to aggression. If loss of life is any index to the value or disvalue of riots, we might recall that the loss of life in the Watts unrest in Los Angeles in one night was greater than that of ten years of nonviolent resistance demonstrations in the Southern part of the United States. Finally, King argued strenuously against the validity of power without conscience, of any claims that power is the goal and that morality is dispensable.

And so this noble disciple of Gandhi, after years of dramatic success, found himself confronted, even in his own ranks, with a philosophy that ran counter to his deepest convictions. He did not retreat, however. Although his idiom became somewhat more insistent in the mid-1960's, he argued his views with passion and continued to pursue his chosen course until, like Gandhi, the assassin's bullet took him from us. What King left behind is a signal contribution to the struggle for freedom and release from indignity. The struggle continues. The demand of the Negro today is as reasonable as that which Diogenes made of Alexander: "Stand out of my sunshine!" This, indeed, is a just demand. Too long has the Negro stood in the shadow—the shadow of slavery, poverty, and contempt. His demand now is that he stand in the full light of human rights.

Gandhi is no longer here to chastise all of us for our discreditable record in race relations nor to say that the unadulterated message of nonviolence may be delivered to the world by the American Negro. But we think we hear his voice and his laughter. We shall remember what he taught us.

NOTES

1. Staughton Lynd, ed., *Nonviolence in America: A Documentary History* (Indianapolis: Bobbs-Merrill, 1966), pp. xv-xvi.
2. Mohandas K. Gandhi, *Non-Violence in Peace and War* (Ahmedabad: Navajivan Publishing House, 1948), 1:113-16, from *Harijan*, March 14, 1936.
3. *Ibid.*, 1:116.
4. *Ibid.*, 1:127-32, from *Harijan*, March 20, 1937.
5. James Farmer, *Freedom, When?* (New York: Random House, 1965).
6. Martin Luther King, Jr., *Stride Toward Freedom* (New York: Harper, 1958), p. 96.
7. Farmer, *Freedom, When?*, pp. 79-80. Italics in the original.
8. Martin Luther King, Jr., *Where Do We Go From Here: Chaos or Community?* (New York: Harper, 1967), p. 52.

9

MAHATMA GANDHI
AND CIVIL DISOBEDIENCE

Paul F. Power

Civil disobedience arises at the boundary between obedience and resistance to the state. It overlaps these two conditions, accepting the system's fundamentals even as it challenges laws or policies. As an identifiable field in political philosophy, civil disobedience is relatively young, emerging only in the last century from theories offered by T. H. Green, Locke and Plato, among others. Thoreau was the first to use the term in the title of his famous essay which explains his refusal to pay Massachusetts poll taxes as a protest against slavery and the Mexican War. Gandhi credited Thoreau as his source for the term and urged the reading of the American's tract. It is not always realized that Gandhi's actual exposure in South Africa to Thoreau's ideas came after Gandhi's first pledge to break a law. In the same way that he related to Leo Tolstoy the Indian leader associated himself with the Yankee individualist as part of an international struggle against injustice. Granting this, one can suggest that Thoreau and Gandhi made significant contributions to making civil disobedience a recognizable subject in political theory.

The development of the topic has been uneven. With the help of studies of Gandhi and Thoreau, but chiefly through traditional perspectives on political obligation, there was progress when analysts examined non-cooperation in German-occupied Europe, neo-Gandhian protest in Britain and India in the 1950's, and the United States civil rights movement. These inquiries stimulated new interest in Gandhi, with Thoreau's revival to follow. Then during the 1960's assertive and unorganized ideas of protest, some of them claiming to uphold civil disobedience, surged through several nations. Although there have been efforts to order and appraise the recent output, conspicuous academic work has used the concept of civil disobedience to radicalize democratic theory.[1] This may be a necessary task, but, in their haste to proceed under the pressures of immediate public controversies, the radical democratic theorists have slighted the job of restoring civil disobedience to the frontier position from which it has slipped or been pushed to the brink of revolutionary theory.

My central assumption is that civil disobedience must be rescued from distortions and manipulations and placed again where it can function as a broker between obedience and revolt. This larger project requires a balancing of radical versions of civil disobedience and neo-conservative objections to all or part of its theory and practice. Despite internal problems, Gandhi's ideas can help to recover *civil* resistance theory. They are not useful solely because of his historical significance, but more importantly because of his insights into certain issues of ethics and power.

Gandhi's version of civil disobedience is part of satyagraha which Pyarelal has called the "diplomacy of truth."[2] The wider framework must be noted to show the relative value of Gandhi's civil disobedience within his pyramid of concerns. One characteristic deserves early mention—the secondary standing of disobedience. The condition is sequential and substantive. Gandhi's civil disobedience is the last method of satyagraha's contest with authority—negotiations and non-cooperation rank ahead in time. Qualitatively, satyagraha is rated below constructive work to end untouchability and to rebuild village life as a preferred way to seek the justice and peace of *sarvodaya*.

Gandhi's civil disobedience has received attention beyond its importance in his thought. Three factors have contributed to the overemphasis. His distinction between illegal civil disobedience through lawbreaking and legal non-cooperation by swadeshi boycotts and disciplined strikes came after his 1906 shift in South Africa from petitioning authorities to disobeying them.[3] Additionally, Gandhi held that when the scope of grievances is restricted in content and place, as in the Bardoli peasant unrest over local taxation, civil disobedience can be used without preparing the atmosphere through constructive work as required in the national campaign for *swaraj.* Thirdly, political analysis tends to focus on the political features of Gandhi's thought and action, thereby stressing Gandhian disobedience at the expense of his metaphysical and social interests. To bear in mind possible exaggerations of the importance of civil disobedience in his total outlook gives a degree of balance to the understanding of Gandhi.

Soundings can now be taken of key premises which shaped Gandhi's view of civil disobedience. In the process, evidence can be accumulated to help decide whether Gandhi's ideas are restorative. The first premise, not limited to Hindu traditions, but prominent among them, is that genuine right is earned, not presumed or seized. The acquisition of merit is crucial for the perfection and self-realization of men and, according to Gandhi, of nations as well. Hindu conceptions influenced, if they did not determine, his understanding of merit. Among them are dharma's insistence on duty ahead of rights, the law of Karma which teaches individual responsibility for the consequences of action, and man's need for penance (tapasya) to make spiritual progress. Gandhi's idea of earned right gives his rule-breaking distinctive qualities of forbearance and self-sacrifice. One can interpret the result as the absorption of social struggle to the psychic plane where there is a resolution of conflict or a haven not available in the outer world. Early in his public life Gandhi rejected this evaluation, with the admission that no political capital should be made out of self-suffering. It is for psychological biographers to answer whether credibility should be given to Gandhi's denial of internalization. For their part, political analysts have found that he made political gains out of self-inflicted suffering, as in his dealings with Ambedkar on the issue of "untouchable" representation. Self-imposed and other-imposed suffering are joined in Gandhi's thought, distinctive as they may be to those who do not accept his way of redemption. Whatever judgment is made of Gandhi's use of fasting for public ends, his version of civil disobedience has a prerequisite of endurance of injustice through non-resistance that eventually qualifies the aggrieved to violate the law under the mantle of earned right. An idea that Marcus Aurelius had meditated upon, endurance is at least part of the justice to which appeal is made. During this time other forms of satyagraha are used, especially negotiations to reconcile the parties. Although Gandhi was not explicit about limits to the non-resistance stage, two are evident. Nehru suggested that there is an internal check, based on the actor's capacity to bear suffering.[4] Gandhi's capacity was considerable; lesser vessels are likely to ask for relief from their burdens. To answer the question, who is to say "enough" for a group, produces an elitist response. The second limit emerges when the acquiring of merit through non-resistance is replaced by an obligation to resist continuing injustice. To persist in non-resistance becomes wrong, because, as Kant explained this point, to abdicate the defense of one's rights violates man's duty to himself. In Gandhi's case the rights are earned; they are not natural in the sense of being immediately operational when challenged. After a time, they become mature enough to justify resistance. Although these two guidelines are imprecise, they give some insight into where non-resistance ends and Gandhian civil disobedience begins.

After civil disobedience starts, fundamental endurance continues through adherence to nonviolence (ahimsa). Here is an important division between Gandhians, who are faithful to ahimsa, and those resisters who would urge or permit psychic or physical injury. Gandhi's endorsement of nonviolent action gives him a prominent place in the traditions of religious reformers with whom he has often been associated—Gautama, Francis of

Assisi and George Fox. In the political history of ethical resisters there are difficulties in finding models comparable to Gandhi. Socrates served in war. Thomas More was king's counsel. Thoreau praised John Brown's violence in a good cause. B. G. Tilak invoked memories of the Mahratta conqueror, Shivaji. Dietrich Bonhoeffer joined a secret network to overthrow Hitler. While Gandhi's elaboration of nonviolent action may not be unique, it is rare in the evolution of resistance ideas where not only coercive doctrines abound but theorists of peaceful change attach qualifications.

The problem of whether a peace theorist is unreservedly committed to nonviolence is an issue for any evaluation of Gandhi's thought. Leaving aside his pre-1919 justification of his non-combattant service in two wars and his recruitment of soldiers for another conflict, the skeptic can ponder Gandhi's response to several tests of his developed pacifism. What is the correct reading, for example, of the 1931 Congress resolution, drafted by Gandhi, that paid tribute to an executed terrorist while disavowing violence, and of his famous 1947 comment that he respected the courage of the Indian Army fighting in Kashmir without mistaking their means for his? Is it accurate to say that Gandhi considered nonviolence his chosen means to pursue truth (*sat*), but other brave and selfless men were entitled to follow their own course? In the past I have been tempted to agree with this understanding. Gandhi's aphorism about his life being an experiment with truth lends weight to the view that he thought that there are several right ways of political action. But a more perfect interpretation of his philosophy emerges if one recalls his belief in (1) a dharmic obligation to seek the final truth; (2) selfless action or duty performed without attachment to rewards (*anāsaktiyoga*), a formula from the Gita, as the best way to pursue the ultimate; (3) courage—spiritual, physical and psychological—as the leading virtue to demonstrate selflessness; and (4) nonviolence "in thought, word and deed" as the optimum form of courage—it is the nearest, temporal approximation to final truth.[5]

The last two beliefs create thickets for political analysts, especially since Gandhi often said that violence is preferable to passivity or cowardice disguised as nonviolence, and that some violence is inescapable in the process of living. Yet, he did not believe that all kinds of fearlessness are acceptable. Courage is evaluated according to the end-in-view, and it, in turn, is joined with the means used. From Gandhi's standpoint, means, at least nonviolent means, are not really means. They are part of a righteous path that is both end and means. There is a basic mistake in assuming or concluding that Gandhi saw nonviolence as a tool, as it is frequently viewed in democratic theory, when he interpreted peaceful "methods" as being ends also. They are ends, because they carry with them the objectives of reconciliation and harmony, not merely a temporary adjustment of conflicting interests. Although he may have confused rightful means with utopian ends, as I believe he did, he denied that he was a visionary. The denial placed him under considerable pressure to prove otherwise. He found an opportunity in social reconstruction and civil disobedience. Nearer to the rigorous Jain view of noninjury than to the elastic interpretations of the Laws of Manu, he taught that for both activities ahimsa, or the law of love, is the highest discipline of the *anāsktiyogi*.

Another difficulty in fully accepting Gandhi as a prophet of nonviolence is based on evidence that in his family and ashram he was frequently a stern moralist. More than one critical observer has said that Gandhi inflicted psychic injury on his wife, sons and other intimates. In his neo-Freudian reading of this evidence, Erik Erikson suggests that it contains implicit violence and that, despite his greatness, Gandhi failed to see the ambivalence of his moral teaching on noninjury.[6] Much can be made of these findings so that the self-righteous, private Gandhi, who was oblivious to the right of autonomous development for those closest to him, becomes in the public arena a leader who preaches nonviolence to impose his own particular and imperfect resolution of inner conflict rather than to open society to the workings of the law of love. Gandhi becomes a leader who injures when he says he heals. My notion for avoiding this conclusion (which I do not believe is true and Professor Erikson does not reach, although his analysis makes it possible) is to look at Gandhi as more prudential and less didactic in the public world than in his household and commune. Evidence of this prudential quality is found in his gradualist outlook on the job of demilitarizing life. Consistent with the slow and painful acquisition of individual merit, the social and political accretion of ahimsa is incremental. Toward the close of his life his response to the coming of nuclear weapons was doctrinaire. But earlier in more representative views, he interpreted the concerns of Western pacifists with a patience that such admirers as Romain Rolland and Muriel Lester in Europe and Richard Gregg and John Haynes Holmes in the United States did not always show in their timetable for the peace movement.

Gradualism in public affairs saves Gandhi's psychological legacy, which may at best be mixed, from invading his legacy for political philosophy, which has no loopholes for war or revolution. In any event, we are discussing a man who, externally studied, would not approve "violence" beyond animal mercy-killing and major surgery. Beyond his case, if there is "implicit violence" in a moralist who is also a political leader, there is a corrective available in the Gandhian tradition, the use of moral pressure against him, a possibility Gandhi himself provided in his opinion that satyagraha can be legitimately employed against one's friends.

A leading criticism of Gandhian nonviolence is that it encourages evil by not resisting with appropriate means. This argument often holds that only when the same values are shared between rulers and resisters will satyagraha work. The key issue here revolves around the nature of the opposing system, especially when it is more stubborn than the British Empire. Although Gandhi contended that sensitive opponents are not a precondition for satyagraha, arguing in 1939 that the Poles could and should have used civil resistance instead of violence against invading Germans, controversies are raised whenever satyagraha is urged against totalitarianism. As with many problems of political ethics, for the short-run one pays one's rupee and makes one's choice. Violence begets violence, Gandhi said, and by insisting on near-term practice of his advice he looked to the long-run when the cycle would be broken. Few would argue with the vision.

Special notice should be taken of Gandhi's complementary teaching—that satyagraha as civil disobedience or in other forms transcends the sterile options of passivity and violence. The process has been interpreted by Joan Bondurant as a dialectical transformation of conflict to a higher level where reconciliation takes place.[7] Here, if nowhere else, Gandhi was innovative. It is difficult to identify a theorist before or since the Indian leader who integrated as well as he did moral constraints and a theory of action. Often either self-discipline or the call for reform is favored, making the doctrine essentially conservative or predominantly radical. Some credit for Gandhi's achievement is due to sacral traditions and British constitutionalism. Both helped to make satyagraha. Mahatma Gandhi provided the critical ingredient. Stated negatively, the contribution of the mix to political ethics is that it avoids both the aquiescence in injustice typical of quietism and the relativism of means found in insurgency.

Overall, Gandhi's version of nonviolence is his signal contribution to the recovery of *civil* disobedience. When the disobedient applies the ethic to himself, his followers and state agents, the process of rule-breaking itself is part of a higher objective, the moralization of social existence through the reduction of violence. The rule-breaker may be only nonviolent because he has been denied other techniques; but he is not Gandhian, although he may have been on the Salt March or participated in a Czech slowdown. The resister might be someone who is nonviolent out of respect for the state's title to a monopoly over violence. He, too, is not Gandhian because of the Mahatma's conviction that there is a reward independent of state theory if one foregoes violence and works for its reduction, even when he is outraged by a public wrong. In the Gandhian liturgy, nonviolence is followed because it is the right thing to do.

The corollaries of Gandhian nonviolence are many and far reaching for the political ethics of civil disobedience. Whether they are all equally creative in rehabilitating disobedience theory is not clear. Willing submission to the legal penalties for the infraction is especially important. Gandhi's adherence to the criterion included his own testimony in 1913 for the Crown's prosecution of a lieutenant. After his arrest for having published allegedly seditious editorials, Gandhi provided a classic example of submission in the Great Trial of March 18, 1922, before Mr. Justice Broomfield in the Ahmedabad Circuit Court, when he pled guilty and proclaimed his reasons for preaching disaffection to the British Empire. That Gandhian submission has its output in publicity and favorable opinion cannot be denied. But these are not the grounds from which it proceeds; the grounds are suffering, as the price for acquiring virtue, and intellectual honesty taken to its logical conclusion.

Gandhi's submission requirement for civil disobedience contrasts with a recent and pronounced trend in resistance thought against the criterion. The current trend includes one or more of the following arguments: Voluntary submission upholds the state's claim of justness which the disobedient has called into question; by his courage to disobey the resister has prepaid the political system for his nonconformity; to submit to penalties is to discredit the logic of disobedience; and acceptance of punishment is testimony in favor of the broken law which is unconstitutional or a policy behind the law that is immoral. The Gandhian reply to all of these is essentially the same—the responsible disobedient is philosophically obligated to accept the consequences of his actions, and, if nothing else, he should demonstrate that he is not an ordinary offender who wants immunity for his misdeeds. If the existential nature of this response has not always been noticed by protesters, the resource is available for consideration by those who reject the submission test through such means as flight from prosecution and demands for amnesty.

An important argument in formal agreement with Gandhian ethics contends that nonviolent civil disobedience is "nonviolent revolution" which ought to receive legal sanction, because it proceeds from moral grounds and seeks to humanize the state.[8]

From this vantage point, the rule-breaker is not only entitled to plead innocent, but the courts should recognize the act's legitimacy and give it formal approval as an advancement in making the state righteous. In relation to this thesis, it is clear that the Gandhian tradition is devoted to humanizing the state. Yet, there is no significant evidence that Gandhi intended his kind of civil disobedience to become a sanctioned civil liberty. Although he derived an ironic message from pleading guilty in British courts, this quality is less vital than his belief that the validity of resistance should not be obscured by the legal permissiveness of the state. To let the state decide that the disobedient act was in fact legal may have its constitutionalist appeal, but the outcome is not Gandhian.

Although no one can speak with certainty as to what Gandhi's outlook on the submission question would be today, his life pattern suggests that his teaching is willing acceptance of penalty even in a society which is not fully democratic. Gandhi's view of submission is contrary to the stand of the insurgent school of civil disobedience in the United States which has divided, and then overshadowed, the traditional libertarians represented by the American Civil Liberties Union. Disobedients are not necessarily following Gandhi's precepts when they invoke symbolic speech under the First Amendment to the United States Constitution as protection for their infractions. Based on his 1906 burning of his Transvaal registration papers, Gandhi's spirit may well have been present when David O'Brien burned his draft card on the Boston Court House steps, but it was not present later when O'Brien sought, unsuccessfully, to find legal immunity for his act. Paradoxically, some of the participants in the 1967 Pentagon demonstrations, which displayed both Gandhian and insurgency tactics, had a grasp of the Indian's ideal when, after arrest for trespass, they pled guilty and either paid their fine or served their sentence.

On balance, there is no need to insist on all features of Gandhian submission to help the recovery of civil disobedience. Recent critics of the criterion are persuasive in so far as they object that a guilty plea is an unwarranted concession to the state's claim of justness. Moreover, I would agree that on the merits of the immunity thesis the state and neutrals should not assume that every challenge to its writ is unprincipled, i.e., criminal. The relief is to be found, however, in the wide discretionary authority of the state to recognize ethical infractions by not prosecuting them, rather than in prejudgment by the disobedients that they are formally as well as substantively innocent. Instead of full Gandhian submission, "responsible" disobedience should require no more and no less than a nonviolent and legal contest within the state's jurisdiction.

In addition to submission, ahimsa requires that those practicing civil disobedience and other kinds of non-cooperation should not take advantage of the opponent's temporary embarrassment. Gandhi withheld a disobedience campaign in South Africa because the Union government had to face a railroad strike. He responded in the same way to British vulnerability in 1914 and 1940. But he reacted differently to the imperial circumstances of 1942, when he launched his "Quit India" campaign. As to the latter reaction, Gandhi violated his own norm.[9] In 1942, Gandhi believed—and objectively it may have been true—that Indian nationalism had reached a desperate point and the 1942 wartime situation offered an opportunity for mass resistance that could not go unexploited. For the master to act against his own principle is not, of course, to deny the validity of the teaching. It is a stringent condition, not easily taught or absorbed. To insist on it is to expect too much of political man.

To this point, is Gandhi's teaching enough to insure the recovery of civil disobedience? Probably not, although it contains a superior ethic that classical liberalism no longer offers and radical democracy has not yet developed. A difficulty in Gandhi's thought is the underdeveloped notion of citizenship. Endowed with a creative integration of moral norm and civic protest, his legacy has little to say about the role of the good citizen in relation to public authority. On citizenship, Gandhi's ideas have a low yield to the point where commentators have spoken frequently of his anarchism. His thought upholds a first duty to God or Truth, ahimsa and one's nation, to name three of the most important subjects in his life-view. Loyalty to the nation does not subsist by itself in Gandhi's political thought. There is a state, only dimly visible to be sure, but it is there. This is the best possible state, taking into account human potential and shortfall. The functions of Gandhi's central authorities are minimal. Increasingly self-reliant tiers extending down from the center through regions to the villages provide the main allocators and communicators of government. Still, the Delhis, Moscows and Washingtons exist not only in a negative sense of abstaining from encroachment on the other levels of the coordinate body, but they perform positive services as well. An example is found in Gandhi's concept of economic stewardship, the godfather of the Congress Government's "social control" of banking, which must have the authorization and the punitive power of the center to have any meaning. Additionally, there is a police force. Gandhians, like Horace Alexander, believe there is no army.

Toward this state the Gandhian citizen has the obligation to be respectful and cooperative. Patriotic fidelity is presumed. Devoted to building individual character and national autonomy and to reducing socio-economic competition and institutional dependency, Gandhi placed no credence in elective processes and delegational structures. Yet, despite the burden on Gandhi to explain what the self-reliant citizen does with his virtues, there is no developed scheme in Gandhi's thought about the citizen's responsibility for the reform and preservation of the polity that makes his autonomy possible. As a consequence, civil disobedience theory can find no special place in Gandhi's political ideas connecting it with the citizen's judgment of the public management of power.

The anti-legal implication of this condition of the good citizen adrift should not be pressed too far. Santhanam has said that "satyagraha can serve as a supplement and in some cases as a substitute" for law.[10] The supplemental function was intended by Gandhi. He did not anticipate the replacement of a system of laws by satyagraha, however necessary the breaking of some rules might become. Although his ideas run counter to the positivist version of the rule of law, they grasp the civic purpose of a statutory network. In the midst of the Rowlatt Act controversy when he was particularly disturbed about imperial legalism, he could still distinguish good statutes that should be obeyed even as he noticed neutral, utilitarian laws that might be broken to protest against the offending legislation on sedition. Discriminations of this kind, joined with his belief in an overriding moral order which compels men and institutions to progress, endorse the ideal of the law in search of itself. Although he became disillusioned with the legal profession, the Indian leader retained some appreciation of the necessity of legislation to approximate the ideal. Because of his long preoccupation with the struggle to replace imperialist rule with national power, he did not expand on how civil disobedience fits into the legal pattern under the conditions of freedom. To the degree that he glimpsed the future, his typical stand held that when the people have national power, dissent should pass through legislative channels; if their needs are frustrated, they have an ultimate appeal to non-cooperation and civil disobedience. He did not foresee how satyagraha would sometimes be distorted in India after his death into anti-legal protest based on specious grounds and using dubious methods. Gandhi should not be held responsible for the postmortem aberrations in India any more than Lincoln should be held liable for distortions contrary to his intentions in American national affairs after his assassination.

Although Gandhi did not offer a comprehensive theory of political obligation, he did suggest answers, which may or may not be acceptable, to two troublesome issues. One appears when rule-breakers go beyond individual consent to make individual conscience the ground of the obligation or right to disobey. The second issue, a variant of the conscience school, rests on the thesis that in case of conflict, one should obey God, not man—the Petrine doctrine. The first justification is vulnerable to the defect of an absolutism of individual conscience, Thoreau's failing. The

Petrine formula, on the other hand, is subject to manipulation, especially if it avoids the risk that Antigone took in disobeying Creon, namely, God's punishment when the rebellion against state law is found to be contrary to divine justice.

Initially, let us examine Gandhi's view of this second approach. Notice may be taken of his stipulation that his true followers should be theists. But should is not must. Not only would a strict application of this rule have excluded some notables like Nehru from Gandhi's circle, but it would have been in conflict with his rejection of political theology. He had a theistic basis for his own rule-breaking; but the evidence points to his general justification of civil disobedience according to the precepts of a moral law governing men (with a few spiritualized exceptions) rather than by God's direct mandate to an individual.

But who is qualified to interpret this law? To consider this question, we must return to the atomic conscience approach. Although Gandhi often referred to the duty or right to disobey laws because of a question of conscience, he did not uphold the "common" individual's conscience as an infallible guide to making a decision between the state's directive and the moral law if they were found in conflict. When a case of possible disobedience arose, determining the right answer was restricted by Gandhi to his own enhanced insight or, at most, to the deliberations of an executive group. Gandhi's tradition speaks forcefully against permitting a decision for disobedience to be made by the ordinary individual. The result is not as oligarchical as it might seem. Together with his semi-monopoly over the authority to decide when civil disobedience is justified, he taught that legitimate lawbreaking is not entered into from superior orders, even his own, and surely not because of contemporary fashion, but out of inner conviction and willing agreement. This voluntarism alone validates the disobedient's act and gives him and the resistance movement the strength to endure and achieve. Noticeable in neo-Gandhian sects led by Danilo Dolci, Martin Luther King, and Albert Luthuli, the rule-breaking formula which Gandhi offered is a blend of elitism and voluntarism.

Gandhi's formula is clarified by something Tolstoy said in a tract which Gandhi urged his followers to read. In dialogue with Russian liberals, Tolstoy advised non-cooperation instead of reform or revolution, both of which, he said, had been found unsuccessful. He went on to discuss the role of conscience in political life. Taking the position that living according to one's conscience is the only way to be influential with others and that only activity directed by one's conscience is useful, the Russian writer commented:

> To say that the most effectual means of achieving the ends toward which revolutionists and liberals are striving, is by activity in accord with their consciences, does not mean that people can begin to live conscientiously in order to achieve those ends. To begin to live conscientiously on purpose to achieve any external ends is impossible. To live according to one's conscience is possible only as a result of firm and clear religious convictions; the beneficent result of these in our external life will inevitably follow.[11]

Tolstoy was more optimistic than Gandhi in believing that every man could develop the proper religious merit that would make conscience a true guide to non-cooperation and civil disobedience. But Gandhi shared Tolstoy's outlook about the error of proceeding directly from the inner light of conscience to right action. Gandhi considered that very few men have the foundations for initiating conscientious disobedience, i.e., religious merit of his degree, which will enable them to authorize lawbreaking in the name of conscience. Yet, the dictate of conscience revealed in public consent would be enough, and, indeed, it would be necessary in order to permit followers to align with the few "great souls" who had glimpsed the truth and authorized disobedience.

For the rehabilitation of civil disobedience, Gandhi's treatment of the conscience problem suggests a mutually limiting relationship between the leader and his constituents, weighed in his favor. The Mahatma's version of civil resistance denies self-certified atomic disobedience. Simultaneously, there is a check on the leader who might find himself a solitary disobedient without convinced followers. The Gandhian set of controls is available to help civil disobedience theory avoid the self-certifying qualities of individualistic models. Whether one requests this help depends on what one thinks generally or specifically of political saints who claim special insight into moral law.

A brief review of this kind cannot evaluate all of the assets and drawbacks of Gandhi's concept of civil disobedience. Important questions that must be left unexplored are the following: What guidelines did he offer for the marshy areas of conspiracy and trespass? Did he wrestle sufficiently with the problems of preventing unintended consequences that might radiate from peaceful lawbreaking? Apart from his own intuitive grasp of what compromises are permissible for the self-respecting disobedient who seeks both reconciliation and justice, are there other suggestions in his tradition which clarify this issue? Does Gandhi's neglect of citizenship mean that he provided no operational linkage between his ethical strategy of conflict and his vision of a perfect society?

Although I am aware that I have not dealt with these questions and their implications for judging Gandhian resistance, I believe that there are some areas in which Gandhi's concept of civil disobedience can be used to reform conflict theory. It would be worthwhile to re-establish the Gandhian distinction between laws and policies which should be resisted and the state agents of those laws and policies who have human rights like other men. Gandhi's idea that illegal action should be grounded on transcendent values and carried out by scrupled means should be continued and applied. Lastly, protest theory must recognize that there may be a choice other than unwilling obedience or political violence. The task of incorporating these ideas into evolving protest theory is considerable. But the project is not impossible, given the transitional stage of political obligation and Gandhi's rank among conflict theorists.

NOTES

1. Christian Bay, "Civil Disobedience: Prerequisite for Democracy in Mass Society," in *Political Theory and Social Change,* ed. David Spitz (New York: Atherton Press, 1967), pp. 163-83; Arnold S. Kaufman, *The Radical Liberal* (New York: Atherton Press, 1968), pp. 56-75; Howard Zinn, *Disobedience and Democracy* (New York: Vintage Books, 1968). An attempt to deal with some issues is my "On Civil Disobedience in Recent American Democratic Thought," *American Political Science Review* 64 (March 1970): 35-47.

2. Pyarelal, *The Last Phase* (Ahmedabad: Navajivan Publishing House, 1965), 1:195.

3. How the emergence of Gandhi's rule-breaking was limited to his community is treated in my "Gandhi and South Africa," *Journal of Modern African Studies* 7 (October 1969): 441-55. The African phase is covered by Vols. 1-12 of *The Collected Works of Mahatma Gandhi* (Delhi: Ministry of Information and Broadcasting, Government of India, 1958-1964).

4. Jawaharlal Nehru, in *Gandhian Outlook and Techniques* (New Delhi: Ministry of Education, Government of India, 1953), p. 15.

5. Gandhi's premises are interpreted in my "Toward a Reassessment of Gandhi's Political Thought," *Western Political Quarterly* 16 (March 1963): 99-108; also, in *Gandhi On World Affairs* (London: Allen and Unwin, 1961), Ch. 2. Different interpretations are found in D. M. Datta, *The Philosophy of Mahatma Gandhi* (Madison: University of Wisconsin Press, 1961); Gopinath Dhawan, *The Political Philosophy of Mahatma Gandhi,* 2nd ed. (Ahmedabad:

Navajivan Publishing House, 1951); and G. Ramachandran and T. K. Mahadevan, eds., *Gandhi: His Relevance For Our Times,* 2nd ed. (New Delhi: Gandhi Peace Foundation, 1967).

6. Erik H. Erikson, *Gandhi's Truth* (New York: W. W. Norton, 1969), pp. 229-54.

7. Joan V. Bondurant, *The Conquest of Violence* (Princeton: Princeton University Press, 1958), especially pp. 196-97.

8. Harrop A. Freeman, ed., *Civil Disobedience* (Santa Barbara: Center for the Study of Democratic Institutions, 1966), pp. 5-6.

9. Arne Naess, "A Systematization of Gandhian Ethics of Conflict Resolution," *The Journal of Conflict Resolution* 2 (June 1958): 150.

10. K. Santhanam, *Satyagraha and the State* (New York: Asia Publishing House, 1960), p. 79.

11. *Tolstoy's Writings on Civil Disobedience and Nonviolence* (New York: New American Library, 1967), p. 154.

10

GANDHIAN SATYAGRAHA AND MACHIAVELLIAN *VIRTÙ*

Anthony Parel

The comparative study of the political ideas of thinkers like Gandhi and Machiavelli, who lived in different epochs of history and in diverse cultural environments, often poses an initial methodological difficulty. For those who hold dogmatic views on the sociological origins of thought and on cultural relativism, these differences may create almost insurmountable barriers. While I do not ignore the relevance of historical sociology to the study of the thought of any great writer, it is important to realize that there are aspects of thought which are of universal significance and which, therefore, lend themselves to comparative study. As Gandhi moves into the main stream of world thought, there will be interest in what is unique in his thought as well as in what is analogous and suggestive in it. Comparative studies become virtually inevitable.

Despite their cultural differences, there are a number of political ideas, such as the nature of political freedom, the function of nationalism or patriotism in the social evolution of a people, the relation between religion and politics, between ends and means, between violence and politics, which are common to Gandhi and Machiavelli. Admittedly, they often disagree on these issues, but to a student of comparative ideas, an analysis of such disagreements can lead to a better understanding of the political ideas of each man.

Space does not allow us to deal with all the themes common to Gandhi and Machiavelli. I have chosen to discuss that of "political action."[1] Neither Gandhi nor Machiavelli is a speculative writer: both were essentially theorists of action, political action. Politics for them was a practical thing, the process of maximum value realization. In the Machiavellian phrase, politics was the pursuit of *verità effettuale* (effective truth) or actual reality. For Gandhi, of course, it was the practice of satyagraha. Despite their appreciation of the importance of action, Gandhi and Machiavelli arrive at different prescriptions for it. This is most obvious on the question of the role of violence in political action. I shall argue here that Machiavelli's pessimism and Gandhi's optimism about human nature and human capabilities lead them to divergent theories of action and of the role of violence which are not mutually exclusive. Indeed, each is incomplete without the other. Thus, I look upon Gandhian satyagraha and Machiavellian *virtù* as alternate and complementary modes of political action.

The key to an understanding of Gandhian views on violence is his moral idealism. He accepted violence as an actual fact, permitted its use sometimes on grounds of political expediency, and condemned it as a moral evil. He was not concerned with a philosophically satisfactory definition of violence but rather with something more important, namely, the reduction of physical violence in the practice of politics. He did, however, make use of legitimizing theories of nonviolence, especially those found in the Gita, the New Testament and certain Jainist texts.

It is possible to express Gandhi's views on violence in the technical language of theory. Man must endeavor to eliminate violence from his practice of politics because nonviolence is more consistent with human nature than violence. In the sphere of voluntary political action only nonviolent political techniques are morally permissible. Socrates is the model of this type of political action: he is the "true soldier." However, when one acts as "man of state," one may be obliged to act according to the dictates of political necessity. The conflict between moral repugnance to the use of violence and the necessity of using it can never be satisfactorily resolved in the present state of man. In trying to resolve this conflict, one's model must be Arjuna. One must perform what duty demands with purity of intention.

Socrates and Arjuna taken together represent Gandhi's attitude towards violence. The essential requirement of Gandhi's moral idealism is the rejection of violence in the sphere of intention. Psychic coercion, unavoidable physical violence, and the sacrifice of one's own life can be tolerated. When the intention is right, one can always find ways and means of reducing physical violence in the practice of politics.

If Gandhi's attitude was guided by moral idealism, that of Machiavelli was guided by political realism. As a thinker, Machiavelli's primary concern was how to make the state strong and stable. This concern was rooted in his humanism. He assumed that the state was necessary for human development and social order, that without the state man necessarily deteriorated in virtue and humanity. In so far as violence maintained the state, it was perfectly legitimate. The following are samples of Machiavellian dicta: the chief foundations of all states are "good arms and good laws. . . . Force and prudence . . . are the might of all governments that ever have been or will be in the world. . . . Good customs without military support suffer the same fate as splendid palaces without roofs. . . . Where peace is necessary, war cannot be abandoned. . . . Armed prophets succeed, unarmed prophets fail."

Machiavelli is not unaware of the moral issues raised by the use of violence. Thus, he sharply distinguishes between violence used for the purposes of state and for private purposes. The former alone is legitimate. Even in the use of violence for purposes of state, Machiavelli distinguishes between modes of use of violence, between well-used and ill-used violence. Violence is ill-used when its application is devoid of prudence and humanity, pity and religion. The prototype of ill-used violence is Agathocles, a Machiavellian version of Duryodhana. Violence is well-used when it is for the sake of the common good and accomplished with the least possible cruelty. The model for well-used violence is Romulus who, like Arjuna, had to engage in a fratricidal conflict. "It is a sound maxim," writes Machiavelli, "that reprehensible actions may be justified by their effects, and that when the effect is good, as it was in the case of Romulus, it always justifies the action. For it is the man who uses violence to spoil things, not the man who uses it to mend them, that is blameworthy."[2]

The reason why Gandhi and Machiavelli take their respective stands on political violence is ultimately because of their views of human nature. Although Gandhi does not speak of a view of human nature in philosophical language, there are elements in his writings out of which it is possible to construct a consistent view. In Gandhi's conception of man there is the triad of man's innate goodness, his actual corruption and the possibility of reform and reconstruction. He speaks of nonviolence as the "law of our species," as violence is the law of the brute. The capacity to know God not only distinguishes man from the brute but also imposes the duty to regulate his life by the norms of nonviolence, i.e., truth and love. The varnashrama dharma was the ideal pattern of society corresponding to this innate goodness.

But historically man has suffered a fall. Speaking of Hindu society, for example, Gandhi says that at some stage of its evolution Hinduism suffered corruption. He gives several explanations for this. The myth of the Yuga is one: historical man finds himself in the Kali Yuga (Black Age). Civilization, or what we might call man's socio-economic environment, is another. Still others are inner factors like desire for immediate gain, unlimited ambition, or fear of one's fellows.

The tendency to corrupt behavior manifests itself in man's ready inclination to adopt brute force as the means to achieve his purposes rather than soul force or nonviolence. In particular, brute force manifests itself in the abuse of the acquisitive and reproductive instincts. As a result of these abuses, both a personal and a social malady affects man. At the personal level, body and soul work in disharmony when the desire for satisfaction of senses conflicts with the spiritual destiny of man. At the social level, the varna system degenerates into the caste system, resulting in the control of the poor by the rich. Wealth and sex, when not governed by the force of truth and love, become the two cardinal sources of human corruption: in Gandhi's phrase, they are "poison." Historical man has become passive about spiritual values and active about material values. He finds himself in a condition in which brute force is, as it were, the new law of action of the fallen man.

However, Gandhi is persuaded that man is capable of self-reform which is historical man's authentic destiny. The task should begin in the soul, but it should end in society. It should produce both inner harmony, personal *swaraj,* and the reform of society, *sarvodaya.* Satyagraha is the means of achieving this twin reform; it is, in effect, political action.

Thus, from a realization of man's actual tendency to corruption Gandhi rises to a vision of human recovery for which right political action is the necessary fulcrum. The task of political reform is not externally achieved by action of the state but rather is the result of man's spiritual transformation. The success of the politics of satyagraha is proportionate to the purity of the soul, to the practice of typically Gandhian virtues like satya, ahimsa, tapasya and brahmacharya. He who attempts to practice satyagraha without the aid of these virtues misunderstands the nature of what he is attempting to do. When an individual, or a group of individuals, becomes transformed interiorly, their resultant action will be peaceful; there will be a reduction of the volume of violence in the practice of voluntary politics. Despite the tendency to corruption, Gandhi views man as still capable of heroic decisions. He makes much of this human capacity for heroism. His doctrine of political action is based on such an assessment of human nature.

Machiavelli, on the other hand, is pessimistic about human nature. His pessimism and the recognition that political violence is the guarantor of public well-being are logically related. Thus, in the *Discourses* he warns his readers that he who wishes to learn the science of government must take it for granted that all men are wicked and that they act right only on compulsion. Similarly in the *Prince,* he advises rulers that they should, if necessary, learn how not to be good. Men are generally selfish, ambitious, ungrateful, deceitful, avaricious, unfaithful. If order and well-being are to be established among beings disposed to manifest these defects in social relations, the rulers should be endowed with a monopoly of force. The political man, in short, is not fully human; he is half-man and half-beast. Political society, consequently, as Machiavelli tells us in the poem the *Ass of Gold,* is like the kingdom of Circe, composed of men who are but beasts in disguise. The art of politics, therefore, partakes of animal cunning and animal ferocity and combines the qualities of the lion and the fox. Chiron, the Centaur, as Machiavelli tells us in the *Prince,* is the true teacher of political science.

The question arises: does Machiavelli deny the effectiveness of moral goodness, what he calls *bontà,* in the practice of politics? The answer is an emphatic "no." His minor writings, in particular his poems and the famous *Exhortation to Penitence,* show us that Machiavelli was quite familiar with the Christian doctrines of sin, repentance, charity and grace. He believed that grace and repentance could cleanse the soul of sin and that man could thereby achieve moral wholesomeness. Indeed, he believed that such moral rectitude was wholly desirable.

But from this he did not draw the conclusion that moral goodness is a sufficient or even necessary ground for external political action. Grace and repentance had a role to play, but only in the inner arena of the soul. Fastings, alms, and prayers and other good works were in themselves good; usury and sins of the flesh (note the similarity between Gandhi's ideas on wealth and sex) were in themselves evil. Machiavelli mentions these things in an explicit reference to his fellow Florentine, the spiritual and political leader Savanarola, the "unarmed prophet," only to dismiss the social theory implicit in the friar's conception of political action. He writes:

> One man, it is true, believes that a deadly thing for kingdoms—what brings about their destruction—is usury or some sin of the flesh, and that the causes of their greatness, which keep them lofty and powerful, are fastings, alms and prayers.[3]

In Machiavelli's view, to say that moral goodness will result in political goodness is political idiocy. Thus, he adds, "to ruin them (kingdoms) such evil is not enough, and not enough to preserve is such good."[4] Machiavelli is not denying the efficacy of moral goodness, but he is denying its claim as a specific means of politics. He distrusts the dependability of human nature to do good. He believes that the man who makes a profession of goodness, among so many who are evil, will necessarily come to ruin himself.

Like Gandhi, Machiavelli also believes in the necessity of social reform through the action of heroic leaders. A corrupt society cannot reform itself: it will need the supreme skill of the rare hero. Moses, Romulus, Lycurgus, among others, are Machiavelli's models. The quality that they require for the task of reform is *virtù*. Thus, surprisingly enough, both Gandhi and Machiavelli agree not only on the need for social reform but also on the fact that its success depends on interior factors—on the purity of intention of the moral act for Gandhi and on *virtù* for Machiavelli. Whereas for Gandhi social reform is the result of the moral reform of the individual, for Machiavelli moral reform and social reform are not causally related. Machiavellian *virtù* is not the result of moral goodness; indeed it is distinct from it, and sometimes may even be directly opposed to it.

Gandhi and Machiavelli are agreed that politics is the means of the effective realization of public values. Spiritual values, however desirable in themselves in the abstract, have no relevance for

Gandhi unless they are put into social practice by those who profess them. For this reason, Gandhi, an intense religious genius, abandons the traditional path of value realization, that of the contemplative sannyasi for a new path, that of a karma yogi in the field of politics. The path is new in the sense that the goal of action is shifted from the purely ascetic practices aiming at individual perfection to that of achieving the common good of the community. Gandhi bridges the gap between religious morality and political morality, a gap which Machiavelli believed essential for the effectiveness of political action.

We may interpret satyagraha as the mobilization of man's latent spiritual capacity, or soul force as Gandhi puts it, to obtain political objectives without, of course, the application of physical violence. As the Mahatma writes, it is a "technique of canalizing the force which is born of Truth and Love or non-violence" by means of exacting spiritual asceticism. Without the continual spiritual exercise of the soul by means of typical Gandhian virtues, satyagraha can never become truly effective. Often the discussion of satyagraha by critics is confined to its technical, external aspects, rules and requirements as though it were just another technique of political action. In my opinion, it is a unique call for utter spiritual purity of intention. The success of satyagraha will depend on this fundamental postulate; without it, what may appear to be satyagraha will in reality be nothing more than *duragraha*.

Significantly, Gandhi often referred to satyagraha as a spiritual warfare, a *dharma yudha,* "in which there are no secrets to be guarded, no scope for cunning and no place for untruth." The spiritual doctrines basic to satyagraha were, of course, derived largely from the Gita. The civil war of the Gita was, for Gandhi, nothing but the civil war in the human psyche. "The real Kurukshetra is the human heart, which is also a dharmakestra."[5] The Pandavas represent the "higher impulses" in man and the Kauravas represent the "baser impulses." "The field of battle is our own body. The eternal battle is going on between the two camps."[6]

The first spiritual condition for the success of satyagraha is the purity of intention. An intention is thought to be pure if the will is free of egoism, and the individual is thus capable of performing duty and avoiding the dictates of self-interest. So long as the will is subject to egoism, the person cannot distinguish between commands of duty and those of self-interest. How is this purity of the will to be attained? In the first instance Gandhi relies on God's grace. "A *dharma yudha* can be waged only in the name of God." In the second instance, however, a pure will is a self-created reality. Voluntarism, in this sense, is the key to the effectiveness of satyagraha. In order that the will may undergo this purification, the person must be prepared to renounce the conventional practices of a purely utilitarian ethic. The liberation of the will requires a conversion of the soul, a radical renouncement of a self-centered life. "Without worrying about the fruit of action," Gandhi tells us, "a man must devote himself to the performance of his duty with an even temper. This is yoga, or *skill in action*."[7]

Freedom from egoism disposes the will to choose the aptest means for the performance of duty. It is in this moral freedom that both the effectiveness of action and the nonviolent character of the means ultimately rest. In the search for the means, the person is not a priori committed to what is suitable to his own self-interest and is, therefore, free to choose whatever is objectively necessary for the action which will be morally good. At the same time, violent means will be automatically rejected by the pure will free from egoism because violence, as Gandhi believes, is the by-product of egoism. "Where there is no desire for fruit, there is no temptation for untruth or *himsa*."[8] It follows that Gandhi does not measure the effectiveness of political action purely by the standards of physical effectiveness. The physical effectiveness cannot be viewed in isolation from the morality of intention and means.

The emphasis on the morality of intention and means may obscure the equally important social aspects of action as seen by

Gandhi. How one passes from a concern for moral purity of the individual will, i.e., from a concern for moral goodness, to political goodness still remains to be seen. Gandhi's explanation is love. The Gandhian individual is not a solipsist who is solely in search of his own personal salvation and moral purity. Gandhi's truth is not only an object of the intellect nor only an object of knowledge; it is something, which, in addition, activates the will and relates the individual to other individuals in a meaningful relationship of duties, obligations, and well-being. Gandhi's truth is known in action.

Because of the social aspects of truth, love is seen as intrinsic to satyagraha, for it is love that makes truth a social reality and achieves the common good. Gandhi thinks that once the individual has undergone the inner change, "has experienced the force of the soul" as he puts it, he will naturally be drawn to the other and to the other-directed action. In other words, the individual will automatically pass from a state of moral freedom to the pursuit of social and political freedom as well. The latter is the proper term of the former.

Now the pursuit of political action involves conflict, no matter how pure the intentions of the actor might be. Gandhi's solution to this problem is very much in the Socratic tradition: it is better to suffer injury than to inflict it on others. According to Jacques Maritain, Gandhi's real genius lies in the systematic organization of patience and voluntary suffering as a special method or technique of political activity.[9]

The idea is that truth and love achieve their maximum social efficacy not with the aid of violence but with that of suffering. This view of suffering, it is good to bear in mind, is essentially a religious view. It is religion which sees a positive value in suffering in terms of atonement, purification, and effective communication. In Christianity as well as in Hinduism, the maximum spiritual efficacy is attributed to suffering. Gandhi transferred this religious means of spiritual effectiveness to the arena of politics. Thus, tapasya emerges as an indispensable means of the efficacy of satyagraha. In practical terms the practice of tapasya means the abjuration of violence in social practice and the adoption of other means, including voluntary suffering, that might result from it. Thus, to take the example of the thief which Gandhi gives in the *Hind Swaraj,* one must treat the thief with love and forebearance if theft as a social offense is to be removed from society. This means the voluntary acceptance of some initial inconveniences on the part of the victim of theft. The victim must voluntarily take the trouble to treat the thief as a brother rather than imprison him. He must help to remove the social and psychological causes that led to stealing in the first place. This is how Gandhi understands the social implication of suffering or tapasya. It is not impractical or masochistic. On the contrary, it calls for a high degree of social awareness and altruism, and its successful application requires a great deal of personal ingenuity and prudence.

It is obvious, then, that the moral idealism on which satyagraha rests can be translated into social reality. The satyagrahi must always be on the lookout for practical ways of expressing his idealism. Gandhi himself discovered many typical symbols, like the charkha, khadi, fasts, etc., which were practical means of conveying his moral values from the pinnacle of aspiration to the reality of action. The use of symbols helps convey the hidden values intended by political action.

Gandhi's use of the spinning wheel has been much misunderstood. Although Tagore regarded it as a symbol of retrogression, in reality it was a means whereby the poor villagers of India could do something to help themselves in the conditions immediately available to them. It was also a means whereby the rich classes could identify themselves, in some measure at least, with their poor brothers. Apart from the economic results that spinning would produce, Gandhi also intended a moral transformation. He did not view the charkha as a "symbol of the rejection of industrialization," as Mr. Arthur Koestler, in a highly misleading and intemperate recent article, opines.[10] Despite Gandhi's statements against the evils of industrialization found in the *Hind Swaraj,* the authentic Gandhian view on economic organization does not reject industrialization as per se evil. Nor was the charkha invented and used by Gandhi to propagate an idea which he did not entertain. Rather, the charkha and its subsidiary symbols were the actual, effective means of contextual political action. If these symbols were irrelevant in a different economic and cultural context, Gandhian satyagraha would not require their use at all. Satyagraha is a creative art, and a practitioner must always display a sense of timing and of context. He must evaluate the traditional symbols in terms of their capacity for communication and effectiveness in producing greater human well-being and community. If the available symbols are found to be wanting, he must discard them and invent his own symbols. The only constants in satyagraha are the love of neighbor, adherence to a pure intention, and other interior virtues. Thus, it would have made no sense had Martin Luther King made the adoption of khadi an essential symbol of his creative adaptation of satyagraha in the United States. On the other hand, he adopted such symbols as were meaningful in the American context, such as voluntary incarceration and the identification of the civil rights worker with the poorer sections of the Negro population.

To sum up, satyagraha as a mode of political action lays equal emphasis on the interior, spiritual purity of the actor and on the technical aspects of action. This interior disposition comprises the freedom of the will from egoism, the mobilization of truth by love, the energization of the imagination and emotions by appropriate symbols, and the voluntary acceptance of suffering as the virute of tapasya would dictate. Political action, for Gandhi, was by emphasis the same as voluntary action. He did not inquire systematically into the grounds of the state's existence and the means whereby it must insure its existence. He recognized the state as a necessary institution and even the reasonableness of using state force to insure public order and security from external threats. He did not systematically integrate these uses of force into a complete theory of nonviolent political action. Strictly speaking Gandhi cannot be criticized for this omission, because he did not intend to give a complete theory of political nonviolence. That is why satyagraha is only one alternative to political action and cannot be viewed as a complete theory of political efficacy.

Turning to Machiavelli, we see that he fills in the gap left by satyagraha. His focus is not the individual so much as the state. For him political action means above all action concerning the purposes of the state dictated by the reason (i.e., interest) of the state. Such action is not voluntary but necessary.

The Machiavellian theory of political action involves three main elements: those of *necessità, fortuna,* and *virtù.* There is first of all the element of *necessità.* The state is an institution necessary for human well-being. Its existence and security are therefore no optional matters. The norm of political action is the success of the undertaking, not so much the morality of the means employed to produce the success. The reason of state is an autonomous value in itself. This means above all that ultimately the question of the state's preservation is not conditioned by the norms of a higher morality which are for the governance of the individual conscience. He who engages in politics, then, must see the proper end of political activity and must distinguish that end from the ends of other types of human activity.

The recognition of the necessary character of political action is only the first step towards achieving political efficacy. The execution of the necessary purpose takes place in a process that is partly within the control of the actor and partly beyond it. *Fortuna* is Machiavelli's term for the area of indetermination and unpredictability. Though the political will is autonomous it is pitted against other wills, equally autonomous, which may frustrate its resolve. Machiavelli uses several symbols to explain the partial unpredictability of political action.

There is first of all the symbol of *fortuna* as a woman. The young and the bold can master a woman. Similarly, a courageous and prudent actor may reduce the chances of unpredictability frustrating his resolves. But then *fortuna* is also like a turbulent river which cannot be successfully dyked. Finally, *fortuna* is like a wheel which signifies the impermanence of circumstances favorable to success. The prudent political actor must take advantage of the right turn of the wheel. In brief, *fortuna* is a co-determinant of political action.

In emphasizing the role of *fortuna* in political action, Machiavelli is in fact only emphasizing the importance of *virtù*. There are two types of *virtù*, heroic and civic. The heroic *virtù* is the efficient cause of political reform or, as the case may be, of original political creation. As a quality of exceptional men, it is a synthesis of prudence, courage, energy, resourcefulness, the ability to act in time and effectively. It is opposed to cowardice, idleness. Its supreme object is the reason of state, and its exercise includes the use of necessary violence. Freedom to use violence when necessary is an important element of *virtù*. Models of those who possessed this quality are, among others, Moses, Romulus, and Lycurgus. Machiavelli called them "armed prophets" in contradistinction to "unarmed prophets" like Savanarola. He believed that armed prophets alone would succeed politically whereas unarmed ones would always fail.

The task of heroic *virtù* is either the founding of a state or the reform of a state already founded but which has fallen into decay. It is the task of the heroic leader to create a community endowed with civic *virtù*, by means of the good arms and good laws, good education and good customs. A people is thought to possess civic *virtù* if they have a sense of unity, patriotism, discipline, and the generosity to subordinate individual interests to the interest of the state. Such a people would be austere in their habits, courageous in battle, and lovers of civic freedom. In existential terms, this means that the natural class antagonisms would be mediated by their common love of the country, i.e., by patriotism. The ancient Romans were such a people. The natural rivalries between the patricians and the plebians never degenerated into a caste system; instead, the nobility gradually incorporated the plebians into their own ranks. This the Romans were able to achieve because of their civic *virtù* which was engendered in them by their heroic leaders.

Now Machiavellian *virtù* differs from Gandhian satyagraha

in at least two respects. First, for Gandhi violence was no part of satyagraha. For Machiavelli, on the other hand, violence was a justifiable element of *virtù*. Secondly, *virtù* and satyagraha differ in their relation to morality. The norm of political action for Machiavelli was the reason of state. True, he distinguished between badly used violence and well used violence in achieving the purposes of the state, but he does not rule out the use of violence on moral grounds. The ultimate reason for this view of political action is the Machiavellian view of human nature. To deal with men who are only half-men, one must learn from the mythical political pedagogue, Chiron the Centaur, and not from the philosopher-king. The Machiavellian political actor must be prepared to take human nature in whatever condition he finds it. The morality and immorality of the means must be judged by their political effectiveness. Machiavelli never says that *virtù* is a substitute for moral goodness; he simply applies to the problem of ethics the fact of political necessity. He feels that if the state is deprived of *virtù*, it is also deprived of its means of existence. This latter can never be; ergo:

> It is often necessary [for a prince] in order to maintain the state, to act against your word, against charity, against kindness, against religion. And so, he must have a mind ready to turn itself according as the winds of fortune and the fluctuations of things command him, and, as I said above, he must not separate himself from the good, if he is able, but he must know how to take up evil, should it become necessary.[11]

For Gandhi, on the other hand, political action was a means of religious fulfillment as well as material welfare. Hence, satyagraha had to be anchored in morality. Sin, in the moral sense, was inadmissible in political behaviour. For Machiavelli, religious morality and political ethic were not causally related. Of course, Machiavelli recognized the place and function of religious morality as his *Exhortation to Penitence* so clearly demonstrates. He detested sin as a moral evil and saw its remedies in grace and repentance (tapasya, if you will). For him, however, grace could never produce political efficacy. He would readily agree, I think, that *virtù* and moral goodness could coexist in the same person at two different levels of personality. For him, man had both religious and political roles to play.

In fairness to Machiavelli, it is necessary to point out that he never morally approves of immoral acts dictated by *virtù*. He did not say that Romulus' killing of his brother, Remus, was a morally good act. All he said was that Romulus was constrained, by reason of state, to commit fratricide which was thought to be politically justifiable. Machiavelli distinguished between virtue and vice, although the distinction had no relevance when the question of reason of state was involved.

In the beginning of this essay we argued that Gandhian satyagraha and Machiavellian *virtù* must be viewed as alternate modes of political action. The reason for this argument must now be clearly stated. Gandhi's assumptions about human nature are as incomplete as Machiavelli's. There are certain capabilities which correspond to the Gandhian vision of man and some which correspond to the Machiavellian vision. Violence in politics would be unnecessary if man were wholly Gandhian. Since man is at least partly Machiavellian, violence becomes necessary for certain types of political efficacy.

Machiavelli did not understand the voluntary aspects of politics. Perhaps in his times politics was understood exclusively as necessary action in the service of a kingdom or a republic. Today the focus of attention has enlarged to include the state as well as the individual and the voluntary groups in the political system. Our notion of the state has also undergone development to the point where the state is seen as having legal or constitutional limitations. Under such conditions, voluntary action can also contribute to the maintenance and security of the state. Satyagraha is no more subversive than *virtù*. In other words, today we have a clearer picture of what political action entails.

In political systems which admit of the limitations of the

state and thus of the validity of the voluntary sphere of political action, satyagraha has an important role to play. But we have not yet reached the point at which it can be demonstrated that the state is unnecessary. So long as the state remains a necessary institution, no matter how narrow and legally circumscribed that area of necessity might be, there will always be the need for *virtù*. Satyagraha and *virtù* together define a theory of complete political action.

NOTES

1. For the purposes of this essay, by "political action" I mean the process whereby public values are effectively realized in a given political system. Action implies the ethical conditions or limitations of action. It implies also the element of voluntarism as well as coercion. Finally, the end of political action must be included: whether action aims at the good of the individual or the state and in case of conflict between the two, which has the primacy.
2. Machiavelli, *Discourses,* in *Machiavelli: Chief Works and Others,* trans. Allan Gilbert (Durham, N.C.: Duke University Press, 1965), 1:218.
3. Machiavelli, *The Ass of Gold,* in *Ibid.,* 2:763-64.
4. *Ibid.,* 2:764.
5. Quoted in V. B. Kher, ed., *In Search of the Supreme* (Ahmedabad: Navajivan Publishing House, 1961-62), 2:231.
6. *Ibid.,* 2:272.
7. *Ibid.,* 2:233. Emphasis added.
8. *Ibid.,* 2:221.
9. Jacques Maritain, *Man and the State* (Chicago: University of Chicago Press, 1951), p. 70.
10. See his "The Yogi and the Commissar," *New York Times Magazine,* October 5, 1969.
11. Machiavelli, *Prince,* in *Machiavelli: Chief Works,* 1:66.